INSIGHT GUIDES

AMSTERDAM

smart guide

Discovery
CHANNEL

APA PUBLICATIONS L

Part of the Langenscheidt Publishing Group

Contents

Below: cycling remains a very popular way to get around.

Left: Amsterdam's famed gables come into view.

Atlas

Below: the tower of the Oude Kerk (see p.38).

Amsterdam

Few cities are as distinctive as Amsterdam. Put the traveller down here, and you could be nowhere else in the world. It is the capital of the Netherlands, but not the seat of government, which is in The Hague, also the Queen's Official Residence. Perhaps this lack of an authority figure has led to its relaxed and tolerant atmosphere, which is just one of its many charms.

Amsterdam Facts and Figures

Population: 750,000 (4.6% of the population of the Netherlands)
Number of bicycles: About 600,000
Number of different nationalities: about 50
Area: 219 sq km (85 sq miles), of which about ¼ is water
Average height above sea level: 2 metres (7ft)
Visitors staying overnight per year: 10 million
Number of prostitutes: 7,000
Number of police officers: 3,600
Number of canals: 165
Number of bridges: 1,200
Number of restaurants: 750
Number of restaurants with Michelin stars: 3

History and Geography

Amsterdam's location means that its history is mainly about its geography. It stands on the edge of a low-lying country, in the place where land merges with lake, river and sea. Amsterdam arose out of a battle between the people and the water, to see who could reclaim and retain the land and survive. In the 13th century the fishing community that had settled here built a dam and a bridge to try to control the shifting River Amstel, and so both founded the city and gave it its name – the Amstel Dam.

The battle with the city's watery foundations goes on, even today. The railway station where most people arrive, the Centraal Station, is built on three artificial islands and supported by stakes. Thousands of wooden piles also support the Koninklijk Paleis, the country's official Royal Palace on Dam Square in the very centre of Amsterdam. The city's beautiful canals can hide dark secrets, and the water must be sluiced out constantly or the city would never survive.

A Tolerant City

Amsterdammers are a fascinating mix of the tolerant and the traditional. Like the rest of the Dutch people, they can be both liberal and conservative at the same time. The city is famous for its relaxed attitude to sex and drugs – prostitution and cannabis are both legal here – but the market for both is primarily the city's visitors, not its inhabitants. Only about 5 percent of Dutch people use drugs, and only about 5 percent of the trade in Amsterdam's notorious Red Light District is from locals. The Dutch are simply more pragmatic than most, and accept that it's impossible – undesirable, even – to try to eradicate man's desires, so it's better to deal with them openly than drive them underground. This aspect of life in Amsterdam can be both shocking and refreshing to the unwary visitor, though you can spend all your time in the city without going near the Red Light District, and hardly aware that you're passing one of the notorious coffeeshops where cannabis is on the menu.

This relaxed attitude is part of Amsterdam's appeal, but so too is its contradictory nature.

Below: a cheerfully decorated bicycle.

Toleration isn't the same as approval, and not all the people who live here are wildly enthusiastic about its reputation for sex and drugs. The laws and social rules concerning both are complex, and it's not a place where you can simply walk along the street smoking a joint. Nor can you make assumptions about what anyone thinks about anything. Luckily, they do like to debate things here, with a strong café society that's based not around coffeeshops but the old bars known as brown cafés.

The Immigrant Mix

In the centre of the city, apart from the mix of Indonesian, Indian and other ethnic restaurants, there is little sign that Amsterdam's population is made up of over 50 different nationalities. About half the city's people now have a non-Dutch background, as its worldwide reputation for tolerance led to many people from overseas coming here to start a new life, especially from the former Dutch trading empire. As you venture further into the suburbs you'll see the city's more cosmopolitan side, with communities of Indonesians, Cambodians, Vietnamese and Surinamese. There are migrant workers from North Africa and Turkey too, and large numbers of Britons, Germans and North Americans living and working in the city. There are inevitable tensions if you look below the surface, but for the average visitor Amsterdam is not only a safe but a stimulating city to visit.

Highlights

▲ **Café culture** Enjoy a coffee, a beer or a smoke in one of Amsterdam's many and varied cafés.

▶ **Anne Frank Huis** It was in this canalside house that Anne Frank and her family tried to hide from the city's Nazi oppressors.

▲ **Begijnhof** In total contrast to Amsterdam's image, this secluded square lined with 15th-century buildings oozes peace and charm.

▶ **Rijksmuseum** This major museum offers an unrivalled collection of works by Rembrandt, Vermeer and other Old Masters.

▲ **Van Gogh Museum** The largest Van Gogh collection in the world, housed in an attractive museum.

▶ **The Canals** A walk, boat tour or bike ride along the canals is quintessentially Amsterdamisch.

City Centre

Amsterdam's city centre, known locally as Centrum, may be only 1km (²/₃ mile) long and 500m (¹/₃ mile) wide, but its skinny cobblestone streets are crammed with fabulous shops, engaging museums and surprising sights such as the tranquil Begijnhof, an oasis of calm in the busy city. At its heart is lively Dam Square, presided over by the elegant Royal Palace (Koninklijk Paleis) and the towering Gothic Nieuwe Kerk. The backbone of Centrum is busy Damrak – which begins at Centraal Station, where most visitors to the city arrive – before becoming Rokin at Dam Square. Running parallel are the pedestrian shopping streets of Kalverstraat and Nieuwendijk.

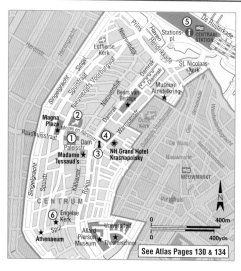

See Atlas Pages 130 & 134

Atop the Royal Palace's enormous domed cupola is a weather vane in the shape of a Cog ship, the symbol of Amsterdam. Beneath the dome are several windows from where one could see the ships arriving at and departing from the harbour.

Dam Square

One of Amsterdam's oldest sites, the enormous public square known as The Dam owes its name to the bridge that was constructed across the **River Amstel** in the 13th century by the fishermen who lived along its banks. The square is watched over by the **Royal Palace** ① to the west, **Nieuwe Kerk** ② in the north-western corner, a branch of **Madame Tussaud's** wax museum on the southern side, and the **National Monument** ③ to the east. Once the site of a bustling central market where Amsterdam's citizens bought their foodstuffs, the Dam is now the location of **Liberation Day** concerts and other events. It is also a popular meeting place, for locals and tourists alike, and attracts an equal measure of buskers, pickpockets and pigeons.
SEE ALSO FESTIVALS AND EVENTS, P.50

Royal Palace (Koninklijk Paleis)

Dominating the western side of Dam Square, the austere Royal Palace was constructed between 1648 and 1665 to designs by celebrated Dutch architect and artist Jacob van Campen. Originally used as a town hall, it was Louis Bonaparte who transformed the sombre building into a majestic palace in 1808. Queen Beatrix holds official receptions at the palace, such as state visits and the New Year reception. Closed for renovations since 2005, it's due to open in 2009 for guided tours.
SEE ALSO PALACES AND HOUSES, P.100

Nieuwe Kerk

Next to the Royal Palace, the Nieuwe Kerk (or New Church) isn't all that new, having been built at the start of the 15th century. It survived three fires, which saw it virtually burnt to the ground, and is now used as a cultural centre and art exhibition space for art and photography – when

6

Left: the National Monument is a popular meeting place.

One of the Netherlands' oldest shopping streets, Kalverstraat, lined with fashion boutiques and shoe stores, may be stylish now, but in the late Middle Ages it was more shabby than chic – it was the main route through the centre for transporting cattle!

not playing hosts to coronations and royal weddings.
SEE ALSO CHURCHES AND SYNAGOGUES, P.38

Around the National Monument

In the square opposite Dam Square, the striking National Monument is another popular meeting place, as the stairs around its base nearly always crowded with weary shoppers. Erected in 1956 to commemorate the loss of lives during World War II, it's the location for annual Remembrance Day services on 4 May. Overlooking the monument are several grand buildings, including the swish department store **De Bijenkorf** ④, and one of Amsterdam's most sumptuous luxury hotels, the **Grand Hotel Krasnapolsky**, which has an

Right: the view over Dam Square from the Royal Palace.

enchanting winter garden.
SEE ALSO HOTELS, P.64; SHOPPING, P.115

Shopping

Running off Dam Square are Amsterdam's busy retail hubs, the hectic pedestrian shopping streets of **Kalverstraat** and **Nieuwendijk**. North of Dam Square on Nieuwendijk are countless stores selling cheap clothes and souvenirs. Closer to **Centraal Station** ⑤,

the shops are edgier, especially around the backpacking area where Nieuwendijk veers toward the **Singelgracht**. In the tiny lanes off the main drag are record stores, esoteric bookshops and stores selling marijuana accessories. South of Dam Square on Kalverstraat are chic fashion boutiques and shoes and accessories shops. The stores become more stylish and upmarket the further south the street goes. Back on Dam Square, behind the Royal Palace, is **Magna Plaza**, an elegant shopping centre in the post office building.
SEE ALSO ARCHITECTURE, P.28

Quiet Spots

The tranquil grassy courtyard of the charming **Begijnhof** ⑥, a 14th-century sanctuary for pious women, is an ideal place to escape the hubbub of the streets, as is the nearby **Spui**, a sunny square in the south of Centrum, a wonderful place to relax and rest weary legs. While tourists can be found enjoying beers on the terrace outside the cafés across the road, local university students can often be found flicking through magazines outside **Athenaeum**, one of the city's best newsstands and bookshops.
SEE ALSO LITERATURE, P.75; PALACES AND HOUSES, P.98

Nieuwmarkt and the Red Light District

The tourist and entertainment area of Nieuwmarkt, with its beer-soaked pubs and fast-food eateries, is immediately east of the City Centre. Whether you're after cutting-edge theatre, Irish bars or girlie shows, you'll find it here. Warmoesstraat and Damstraat are the ground zero of bars and coffeeshops, with the area becoming increasingly hipper around Oude Hoogstraat and Nieuwe Hoogstraat, an area popular with arts students. North is Nieuwmarkt Square, Chinatown and the Red Light District.

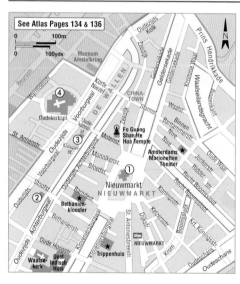

The Zeedijk, or 'sea dyke', dates from the Middle Ages, when it protected Amsterdam from the waters of the Zuiderzee, an inlet to the North Sea. Stand at an intersection and squat down and you'll see the little street is raised slightly higher than those surrounding it. In the 17th century, the Zeedijk was a highly desirable place to live and one of the most respectable residential streets for a successful merchant.

Nieuwmarkt

Laid-back, leafy Nieuwmarkt square is, somewhat surprisingly, at the centre of a small but boisterous district that is now Amsterdam's seedy entertainment zone, with something to please everyone. There are dimly lit Irish bars and neon-lit brothels for boys on stag nights, rowdy music venues and smoky coffeeshops for the backpacker crowd, and sunny café terraces with boutique beers on tap for more mature visitors.

In the surrounding streets there are many greasy takeaways to soak up the booze.

As you'd expect from such a wild neighbourhood, the district also has a rather notorious past. In the 1970s, it was the setting for the Nieuwmarkttrellen (Nieuwmarkt riots), a massive public protest against the development of a subway line. During World War II, the German occupiers used it as an assembly point for the deportation of Amsterdam's Jews. During its 400 years, Nieuwmarkt square has been home to a regular market, and now is home to a Saturday farmers' market and a Sunday antiques market.

Now a wonderful café with an atmospheric interior, **De Waag** ①, or the Waaggebouw or 'weigh house', is the most prominent building on Nieuwmarkt square. Once part of the late 15th-century city walls, it was the eastern gate to the city, but following Amsterdam's expansion at the start of the 17th century, it was rebuilt as a freestanding weigh house. Over the years various guilds have been housed here, among them blacksmiths, bricklayers and painters.

SEE ALSO PALACES AND HOUSES, P.101

Left: an infamous sight in the Red Light District.

nese and other Asian eateries, as well as Asian food shops, is on the **Zeedijk**, or 'sea dyke', the main street of Chinatown *(see box, left)*. Here you'll also find the somewhat incongruously located Buddhist temple, in a traditional Chinese courtyard style of architecture, a tranquil haven in an otherwise raucous neighbourhood.

Oude Kerk

The **Oude Kerk** ④, or Old Church, is located west of Nieuwmarkt and was built around 1250. It was originally a Catholic church, but was transformed into a Protestant church some time after 1578 following the Reformation. The Oude Kerk was much more than a church: along with the square outside it was a meeting place for Amsterdam's citizens and traders visiting the city on business. Many of Amsterdam's citizens were buried here, including Rembrandt's first wife. These days, it's used as an exhibition space for art and photography and is the venue of the famous **World Press Photo** exhibition each year.

SEE ALSO CHURCHES AND SYNAGOGUES, P.38; FESTIVALS AND EVENTS, P.50

Red Light District

The Red Light District, or *De Wallen* as it's known locally, is a compact area of strip clubs, brothels, sex shops and working girls in windows. It's said that the 'world's oldest profession' has been practised in this area since medieval times. The Red Light District takes in the canals of **Oudezijds Voorburgwal** and **Achterburgwal** and the lanes that run between them, such as Trompettersteeg, so narrow it's hard to pass oncoming pedestrians without touching. The semi-clad women (generally wearing lingerie only) reclining on sofas in windows – some the front rooms of canal houses, others no larger than a phone booth – are what most tourists come to see. There were around 400 'windows' in operation, but the numbers have dropped in recent years and are being reduced further, largely due to the gentrification of the area,

which is becoming increasingly hip in pockets, but also due to social efforts to buy the properties and curb prostitution. Studies have revealed that most of the women are managed by pimps (something the windows were intended to prevent) and many have been trafficked here, from Africa or former Soviet Union countries. The neighbourhood is also home to quirky museums such as the **Hash, Marihuana and Hemp Museum** ② with its intriguing exhibition on the history of cannabis, and, naturally, an **Erotic Museum** ③.

SEE ALSO MUSEUMS AND GALLERIES, P.79

Chinatown

While there are Chinese restaurants scattered all over the Nieuwmarkt area, the largest concentration of Chi-

Right: the atmospheric interior of the Oude Kerk.

Western Canal Belt and the Jordaan

West of the city centre, the stylish Western Canal Belt and atmospheric Jordaan are some of the loveliest parts of Amsterdam, with their canalside houses, leafy lanes and romantic bridges decorated with flowerpots. The area boasts some of Amsterdam's engaging museums, including the Anne Frank Huis. It's also home to the chic 'Nine Streets' area, the city's best shopping quarter, with lovely cobblestone lanes. There are also pedal boats for hire opposite Westerkerk, so you can see the area from the water.

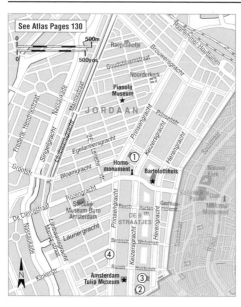

As you explore the area, you'll find yourself passing a striking monument beside the Westerkerk, Amsterdam's Gay Monument, the **Homomonument**. Comprised of three pink granite triangles that are connected by one larger triangle, the design confounds many passers-by. The source of inspiration dates back to World War II, when homosexuals in concentration camps were forced to wear a pink triangle.

bridges. In summer, the area is lively with locals taking advantage of the sunshine.

The Nine Streets

The 'Nine Streets' or *De 9 Straatjes* connecting the canals include **Reestraat**, **Hartenstraat**, **Gasthuismolensteeg**, **Berenstraat**, **Wolvenstraat**, **Oude Spiegelstraat**, **Runstraat**, **Huidenstraat** and **Wijde Heisteeg**. This laid-back shopping area has a village feel to it. Shopkeepers sit outside their stores and read a book when business is quiet, and in the summer evenings they'll share a bottle of wine as shoppers browse. This is the place for one-of-a-kind shops, from stores specialising in antique eyewear to toothbrushes, and

Western Canal Belt

Taking in the beautiful canals of **Herengracht**, **Keizersgracht** and **Prinsengracht**, and the charming streets that connect them, the Western Canal Belt is the area responsible for giving Amsterdam the name the 'Venice of the North'. The canals were constructed at the beginning of the 17th century as part of a major development plan aimed at creating more space

for the city's rapidly expanding population, and it was largely the well-heeled who moved into the elegant mansions and grand canal houses that lined the waterways. Even now, the houses are either the private homes or offices of the city's well-off citizens.

The canals' streets are sprinkled with restaurants, cafés and bars, with wooden benches out front, chairs by the water and tables on the

Left: a tour boat glides through the Western Canal Belt.

original residents out. In the 1960s, artists, craftsmen and students resided here, but in recent decades it has become more gentrified by wealthier citizens, although it is still home to artists and retains a lively and unique atmosphere.

Museums

Home to many excellent museums, the area teems with tourists, and is best visited early in the morning or in the evening to avoid the crowds. There is the **Anne Frank Huis** ①, the building where the Frank family hid in a secret apartment during the German occupation from 1942 to 1944, the **Huis Marseille** ②, a superb photography museum located in a beautifully restored 17th-century building, and the fascinating **Biblical Museum** (Bijbels Museum) ③. There are also some quirky places, including the **Houseboat Museum** (Woonbootmuseum) ④ and the delightful **Amsterdam Tulip Museum**.
SEE ALSO MUSEUMS AND GALLERIES, P.80, 81

it's also home to Amsterdam's more alternative fashion boutiques, quality handmade leather goods, rare book stores and contemporary art galleries. Meanwhile, there are stylish cafés and bars, old-fashioned tearooms, and excellent restaurants for when you need to rest and refuel.
SEE ALSO SHOPPING, P.114

The Jordaan

Bordered by the **Brouwersgracht**, **Raamstraat**, **Lijnbaansgracht** and **Prinsengracht** canals, the

Jordaan was part of the same major 17th-century development project as the Western Canal Belt that saw the city expanded to make way for the growing population. However, the Jordaan was created for the working class, which explains why the houses are smaller and narrower. As a result of overpopulation and poor sanitation in the 18th century the area became run-down, and in the 20th century many buildings were demolished and new houses constructed, forcing many of the

The origin of the Jordaan's name is often disputed. Some argue it was derived from the French word for garden, *jardin*, which Amsterdammers adapted to Jordaan. This can be explained by the fact that it's one of Amsterdam's leafiest areas, with lovely trees and flowerpots on the bridges. Others argue that its name was derived from the River Jordan in the Middle East, because the Jordaan was a working-class district that was home to immigrants who saw the wealthier neighbourhood on the other side of the Prinsengracht as the 'Promised Land'.

Below: shopping in the Nine Streets district.

Southern Canal Belt and Leidseplein

The 17th- and 18th-century gabled houses lining the the Southern Canal Belt are among Amsterdam's grandest and prettiest, offset by attractive arched bridges, locals going about their daily business by bicycle, and flower-filled houseboats. The floating Bloemenmarkt, feline-themed Kattenkabinet and impressive Stadsarchief building all add to the noble air. In contrast, the busy Leidseplein is Amsterdam's entertainment hub and nightlife centre, with more cinemas, clubs and restaurants than anywhere else in the city.

Around the Golden Bend

Many visitors to Amsterdam will simply pass straight through the Southern Canal Belt on their way from the City Centre to Leidseplein and Museum Quarter (see p.16). Those who do linger for more than a passing glance are in for a treat. During Amsterdam's rapid expansion in the 17th century, **Herengracht** quickly became the most desirable of the three newly constructed canals. Where it turns southeast at **Leidsegracht** and east just before **Vijzelstraat**, house-buyers on Herengracht were encouraged to buy two lots and build double-fronted mansions. As a result, the richest of well-to-do merchants homed in to build their city palaces with classicist facades, stuccoed ceilings and fine gardens, hence the name **'Golden Bend'** ①. Check out Herengracht 475 and 476 for the most elabo-

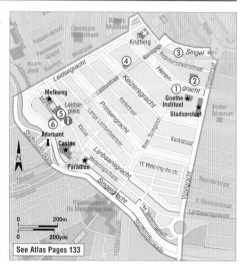

See Atlas Pages 133

The Leidseplein originally developed in the 17th century as a wagon park where farmers and peasants could leave their carts before entering the city centre. The name derives from Leidsepoort, the name given to the Amsterdam end of the main road from Leiden.

rate. Many are opened to the public once a year.

Nowadays, most of the buildings are occupied by banks, offices and some cultural institutions such as the **Goethe Institute** and the **Kattenkabinet** ②, an art museum on the Herengracht canal devoted to works depicting cats. The collection includes works by Picasso, Rembrandt, Toulouse-Lautrec, Corneille and Sal Meijer, among others.

The chequerboard **Stadsarchief** building, on

Vijzelstraat, is home to the city's archives – the largest municipal archive in the world. Formerly the home of the Dutch Trading Company, the building's resplendent facade is most noted for the carvings on the corners of the building that represent the continents the trading company's dealings straddled.
SEE ALSO ARCHITECTURE, P.28; MUSEUMS AND GALLERIES, P.82

Flower Market

Located on the **Singel** canal between the Koningsplein

Left: alfresco café culture in the Leidseplein.

theatre), which dominates the square and serves up high-brow homegrown and international dance and theatre.

Live entertainment venue **The Lido** is popular, whilst the streets radiating off the square offer restaurants serving all manner of international cuisines, with set menus that vie to offer the best value for tourists. The **casino** and music centres **Paradiso** and **Melkweg** are also located here. Just off the square in the Ledsebos is the intriguing **Adamant**, a hologram effect sculpture erected in 1986 to celebrate the 400 years of the city's diamond trade.
SEE ALSO MUSIC, P.92; NIGHTLIFE, P.94; THEATRE AND DANCE, P.122

Café Culture

Leidseplein's café culture dates back as far as the early 19th century when the city's first terrace bar opened, the Café du Théâtre. Demolished in 1877, the café was replaced by the Art Nouveau magnificence of the **Eden Amsterdam American Hotel** ⑥ on the southwest corner of the square. The hotel's **Café Americain** is now the place to see and be seen in, whilst enjoying a coffee and a cake.
SEE ALSO BARS AND CAFÉS, P.33; HOTELS, P.67

and the Muntplein is the **Bloemenmarkt** ③, the only floating flower market in the world. A fragrant feast for the senses, the market is actually made up of a series of houseboats crammed full of floral displays that spill onto the pavements in front to offer locals and visitors alike a gigantic assortment of flowers, bulbs, plants and gifts. The ideal location to wander and soak up the atmosphere, this is one uniquely Dutch experience.
SEE ALSO MARKETS, P.77

Leidsestraat

Follow the Keizersgracht canal westwards from the Stadsarchief and you'll come across the frenzied, tram-filled Leidsestraat. The main route from the Golden Bend down to the bustling Leidse-plein, this thoroughfare is home to designer department store **Metz and co** ④ and numerous other mid-

range, big-name stores. Sprinkled on and around these streets are wonderful little eateries, great for a quick bite and a refreshing drink. Pound these pavements and you won't walk away empty-handed.
SEE ALSO SHOPPING, P.115

The Leidseplein

At the end of the Leidsestraat lies **Leidseplein**, an L-shaped 'square' that's now one of Amsterdam's most popular centres for nightlife. Jugglers, street musicians, fire-eaters and other performers make the square a lively place until the early hours, especially on warm summer evenings. During the day, throngs of merrymakers soak up the atmosphere from the pavement cafés, under the shadow of the **Stads-schouwburg** ⑤ (municipal

Right: flowers for sale at the Bloemenmarkt.

13

Eastern Canal Belt and Rembrandtplein

Sandwiched between the Vijzelstraat to the west and the mighty River Amstel to the north and east, the Eastern Canal Belt marks the last stage of the city's 17th-century canal construction programme. An area of contradictions, with immaculately preserved historic houses on peaceful streets and an abundance of lesser-known top-class museums sitting alongside the hedonism of lively squares such as Rembrandtplein and Thorbeckeplein, no area better demonstrates the broad-mindedness of Amsterdam.

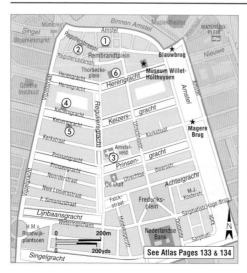

See Atlas Pages 133 & 134

Around Rembrandtplein

Unfailingly lively any night of the year is the unashamedly tawdry **Rembrandtplein**. Originally part of the 16th-century ramparts, the square took its name in 1876 following the erection of a statue of Dutch Master Rembrandt, which sits in the centre of the square gazing towards the old Jewish Quarter, **Jodenbuurt** *(see p.18)* beyond. From topless bars to vast nightclubs with all other forms of licensed establishment in between,

Rembrandtplein is very commercialised, boasting delights such as Europe's largest digital screen, on the face of the **Escape** 'super-club' ①, along with numerous obligatory souvenir shops. Commercialisation does bring one benefit, however – the ability to people-watch – with a prime seat in one of the square's cafés a great location from which to enjoy the passing sights.

Beyond the commercialisation there are some gems (as well as the reputable

diamond dealers located here!) to be enjoyed, such as the 22 bronze figures that make up a three-dimensional replica of Rembrandt's most famous piece, *The Night Watch*. To the northwest of the square, heading up Reguliersbreestraat, the **Pathé Tuschinski Theatre** ② cinema won't disappoint thanks to a decadent Art Deco interior and wonderfully ornate facade, coupled with an eclectic screenings schedule. Preserved and restored to its former glory, it is worth joining a guided tour in the summer months. SEE ALSO FILM, P.53; NIGHTLIFE, P.94

Thorbeckeplein

Off the south side of Rembrandtplein lies the cobblestoned, shady space of contradictions called **Thorbeckeplein**. Circled by hotels, cafés and restaurants, it's a busy spot, where every Sunday between mid-March and October visitors will happen upon a sophisticated little **art market** that is somewhat incongruous amongst the surrounding topless bars. The centre of the square plays host to a statue of J.R. Thorbecke, the man

Left: the bright lights of the Rembrandtplein at night.

ings, porcelain, silver and other valuable items, located in a building restored to replicate how the house was in the 18th century. **Museum Willet-Holthuysen**, found on the Herengracht, offers an insight into life in a bygone age through a house that has been preserved in its original state.

The **Tassenmuseum Hendrikje** (Museum of Bags and Purses) ⑥ on Herengracht doesn't require any explanation, although it is worth mentioning that the collection covers the Middle Ages to today, including specimens such as one of Madonna's handbags! See also Museums and Galleries, p.83, 84

The Reguliersgracht canal is famous for its seven hump-backed bridges, which gave the **Seven Bridges Jazz Festival** its name. The only free jazz festival in Amsterdam, the event takes place at various venues along the canal every September.

---

responsible for the Netherlands' 1848 constitution – another bizarre placing given his serious work against the carefree abandon represented by the establishments here.

The Amstelkerk

Due south of Thorbeckeplein, on the **Prinsengracht**, lies the wooden church of **Amstelkerk** ③. Designed by Amsterdam Master Builder Daniel Stalpaert in the late 17th century as a preacher's barn, it was assumed that a permanent church would eventually replace it. Today, locals are still waiting for this

to happen. Restored in 1988, the church enjoys a picture-postcard setting in the wide-open spaces of the **Amstelveld Square**, providing a welcome haven of calm if the excesses of Rembrandtplein prove too much.

Museums

Home to a number of outstanding museums, yet often overlooked by tourists, the Eastern Canal Belt is generally an area where there's no need to get up early to beat the crowds. **Foam** ④ is a small but influential photographic gallery on Keizersgracht that acts as a meeting point for the city's creative photographers. **Museum van Loon** ⑤, also on the Keizersgracht, is a sumptuous arts museum featuring furniture, paint-

Right: part of the bronze replica of Rembrandt's *The Night Watch.*

15 Bridges

If peace and quiet is more your thing, **Reguliersgracht** is one of Amsterdam's most peaceful canals. At the intersection of the Herengracht and Reguliersgracht, tourists gather to try to spot the **15 bridges** allegedly within view. Most easily achieved in winter when the trees have shed their leaves, the view really does live up to the hype.

The Museum Quarter, Vondelpark and the South

The Museum Quarter, Amsterdam's cultural hub, plays host to three of the finest museums in the world, crammed full of priceless exhibits from Dutch Masters such as Rembrandt and Van Gogh, with the odd Picasso and Warhol thrown in for good measure. To the east of the district lies the Vondelpark, a haven of open space, in the residential Old South. Further south, parks and business centres can be found in the New South and Amstelveen, two suburban neighbourhoods.

The Museum Quarter

Nestled south of the bustling Leidseplein is the elegant 19th-century Museum Quarter. At its heart lies the **Museumplein**, the wide-open space that links the three big museums. Redeveloped at the turn of the century by Swedish landscape architect Sven-Ingar Andersson, the grand, grassy areas extend unbroken from museum to museum, with colourful benches, skate parks and basketball courts all adding life to the open space without being intrusive. Underground garages keep the hordes of tour buses and cars out of sight, and frequent events are held on the Museumplein.

For art-lovers, the coming years are sadly not going to be ideal. The **Rijksmuseum** ① is currently closed for refurbishment, with the latest estimates suggesting reopening won't take place until 2013. Until then, only the 'greatest hits' of the monumental collection are on display, although that still means you'll see the likes of Rembrandt's *The Night Watch*, along with works by other Dutch Masters such as Vermeer and Steen. The situation at the **Stedelijk Museum** ② doesn't look much better either, with the different displays of art from names such as Picasso, Matisse and Warhol to be displayed at various venues around the city such as the Nieuwe Kerk *(see Churches and Synagogues, p.38)*. That leaves the **Van Gogh Museum** ③, which of course is no hardship, with over 200 paintings and 600 drawings by the revered man on show. One of his most famous works, *Sunflowers*, takes pride of place.
SEE ALSO MUSEUMS AND GALLERIES, P.85

Concertgebouw

With acoustics reputed to be as good as you'll get anywhere in the world, Amsterdam's **Concertgebouw** ④ (concert hall), located towards the southern end of the Museumplein, is a stunning venue in

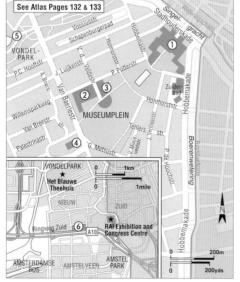

See Atlas Pages 132 & 133

Right: relaxing in the green space of the Vondelpark.

Left: the Rijksmuseum dominates the Museumplein.

of the park forms a popular meeting point for a refreshing cappuccino or something colder, whilst the **Nederlands Filmmuseum** ⑤ at the north-east corner is of note because of its work in finding, restoring and promoting film treasures. SEE ALSO BARS AND CAFÉS, P.34; FILM, P.53; PARKS AND GARDENS, P.105

The South

Whilst the houses on the bohemian streets of the Old South (Oud Zuid) around the park contrast with smarter equivalents up by the muse-ums, the further into the New South (Nieuw Zuid) you go, the more modern the buildings become. Any character of note can be found around **Beethovenstraat**, although most visitors to this area will be heading to the **World Trade Centre** ⑥ on business or to the behemoth that is the **RAI Exhibition and Congress Centre**, which hosts some big-name concerts and exhib-itions. The **Beatrixpark**, named after the Dutch queen and more recently extended and renovated, is worth a visit, with the Victorian walled gar-den a masterpiece of its time. Further south, **Amstelpark**, built for the 1972 Floriade garden festival, is a fair bet if you fancy a meander through beautifully manicured gardens. SEE ALSO PARKS AND GARDENS, P.102

which to take in a classical music concert. One of the world's most beautiful concert halls, it's no wonder the list of composers who have held court reads like a who's who of classical music. With the biggest names in classical music making an appearance over the years and relatively inexpensive ticket prices, few places offer a more cultured way to round off the day. SEE ALSO MUSIC, P.90

Vondelpark

Of Amsterdam's 30 listed parks, few come close to matching the magic of the bohemian-flavoured **Vondel-park**. Aptly named after city poet Joost van den Vondel, whose play Lucifer caused the religious powers of the day to crack down on 'notorious liv-ing', the park today throngs to the tune of bongo players, who ramp up the atmosphere amongst the dope-tokers and dog-walkers. Interestingly, the park is actually sinking, with some of the larger trees float-ing on polystyrene blocks and the ponds and lakes full to the brim. The **Blauwe Theehuis** (Blue Teahouse) at the centre

The southern suburb of Amstelveen allows visitors to catch a glimpse of everyday life for the majority of the city's population. Often overlooked is the **Amsterdamse Bos**, despite offering some wonder-ful sights and open spaces. *See also Parks and Gardens, p.102.*

Jodenbuurt, the Plantage and the Oost

To the southeast of the City Centre is the charming, if curious, mix of old and new that makes up the Jewish Quarter of Jodenbuurt. After the Jewish population was dramatically reduced during World War II, the area descended into neglect, prompting a period of demolition and property development. Despite this, the area is still a fascinating memorial to the past, offering plenty to see and do. Life revolves around the Waterlooplein, whilst further afield the extensive Plantage park and the Oost merit exploration.

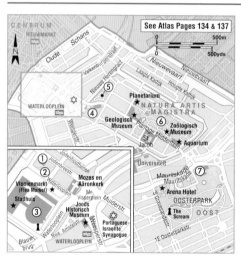

Synagogue and the **Joods Historisch Museum** reveal much about the once-sizeable Jewish population in Jodenbuurt. Jews from all over Europe fled to the relatively tolerant Amsterdam from the 16th century onwards; by the time the Netherlands was occupied by the Nazis in 1940, around 10 percent of Amsterdam's population was Jewish. Only about 5,000 of these, 1 in 16, survived World War II.

SEE ALSO CHURCHES AND SYNAGOGUES, P.39; MARKETS, P.77; MUSEUMS AND GALLERIES, P.86, 87

Amsterdam's Gems

Amsterdam's diamond trade was historically dominated by Jewish families (for centuries, it was one of the few trades open to Jews, as it was not controlled by the guilds), and in the area stretching from Jodenbreestraat towards the harbour, visitors will come across a maze of back alleys that once housed numerous diamond polishers and cutters. Today, **Gassan Diamonds** (173 Nieuwe Uilenburgergracht), welcomes visitors to have a look at the various processes involved in the diamond process. Located in the former Boas diamond-polishing factory,

Jodenbuurt

Most tourists commence their exploration of the Jodenbuurt from the modern setting of the **Waterlooplein**. Located in the northeast corner of the neighbourhood and fringed on three sides by water, the square is home to the 300-stall **Waterlooplein Market**, where visitors brave enough

Waterlooplein takes its name from the Battle of Waterloo, during which Dutch troops played a prominent part in the defeat of Napoleon.

to have a root around can pick up a genuine bargain. Of note is the Roman Catholic **Mozes en Aäronkerk**, whilst **Rembrandthuis** ① is a fascinating museum and the city's only surviving building from the 17th century. Next door is the **Holland Experience** ②, a modern three-dimensional trip through the Dutch landscape that Rembrandt loved. It is hard to imagine what the Old Master would make of it.

On the western side of Waterlooplein, the **Portuguese-Israelite**

Left: the glasshouse at the Hortus Botanicus.

known as **Artis Zoo** ⑥, it was established in 1838, making it the oldest zoo on the European Continent. Here you can admire animals from all corners of the world. Also found here are the **Geological Museum**, **Zoological Museum**, greenhouses, an **Aquarium** and a **Planetarium**, the elements that make up the 'Museum of Life' that is Artis.

SEE ALSO CHILDREN, P.36; PARKS AND GARDENS, P.104

The Oost

To the south, just over Mauritskade, is the Oost, home of the **Arena** hotel, restaurant and nightclub trio, housed in a former Catholic orphanage. Just south of here is the **Oosterpark**, a former graveyard turned green space. Look out for *The Scream*, a sculpture erected recently to commemorate the murder of outspoken film director Theo van Gogh. The interesting **Tropical Museum** (Tropenmuseum) ⑦ is worth checking out, but the most common pursuit here is passing the time of the day wandering around the lakes or picnicking whilst admiring the birdlife.

SEE ALSO FILM, P.52; HOTELS, P.69; MUSEUMS AND GALLERIES, P.88; PARKS AND GARDENS, P.104

As a melancholic reminder of the ravaged past glories of the Jewish Quarter and its subsequent demolition to make room for new development, a demolition ball is on display at Waterlooplein metro station. Look out for it as you pass through.

---

which was founded on the same spot in 1878, it is a fascinating sight.

Opera and Dance

On the banks of the Amstel in Waterlooplein is the modern **Muziektheater** ③, which is the home of the **Netherlands Opera** and the **National Ballet**, and is loved more for what goes on inside than for its appearance. Many performances sell out rapidly, so book well in advance if you intend to take in some of the finest productions found anywhere in Europe.

SEE ALSO MUSIC, P.91; THEATRE AND DANCE, P.123

The Plantage

Cross over the **Nieuwe Herengract** from Waterlooplein and you'll instantly discover why this area lives up to its name of the 'Plantation District'. The **Hortus Botanicus** ④ is a green oasis of peace and quiet, established by a group of well-to-do merchants in the 17th century. They felt the need for a garden, so set about creating a herb garden for physicians that was also a pleasure garden for locals. Over the years the collection has developed, with a unique collection of plants.

Located a short distance to the north is the **Holocaust Memorial** ⑤, whilst further east is the area's most popular attraction, namely **Natura Artis Magistra** ('Nature is the Mistress of Art'). Better-

Right: sombre displays of remembrance at the Joods Historisch Museum.

The Waterfront

Amsterdam owes much of its history and wealth to its Waterfront district. It was here that Dutch maritime expertise blossomed, firstly through fishing and then through trade with the Far East and Americas, which made Amsterdam's port so busy in the 'Golden Age' of the 17th century. Today, the Waterfront offers a reminder of that past success, with the warehouses, quays and museum ships of yesteryear standing tall alongside modern-day attractions such as NEMO and the Muziekgebouw. For visitors looking to grasp an understanding of where the city's history began as well as today's architectural developments in Amsterdam, this area warrants exploration.

Along the Waterfront

Despite something of a forlorn appearance these days, Amsterdam's waterfront is still an interesting place to explore for a few hours. Dominated to the north by the **IJhaven**, the main waterway full of toing and froing barges, cargo boats and passenger boats, the area is often the first port of call for many visitors thanks to the recent development of the city's **Passenger Terminal** ①. Designed to house the ever-increasing size and number of cruise ships mooring in Amsterdam, the new terminal houses a convention centre, restaurants, banks and shops in a development that echoes the overall theme of the area – modernisation at a rate of knots not seen since the Golden Age of booming trade and commerce. This part of town is also a good place to pick up

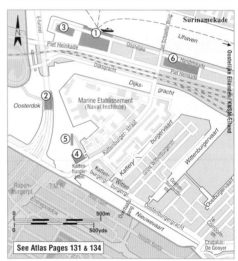

See Atlas Pages 131 & 134

As NEMO is built over the top of the IJ Road Tunnel, a few quirky features had to be included. The most noticeable is to do with the foundations – because the tunnel is curved, NEMO had to follow suit with the same curves mirrored above ground.

one of the many passenger boats that ferry visitors to the **Eastern Islands** (Oostelijke Eilanden). Of particular interest, and accessible by bridge as well as ferry, are **Java-Eiland** and **KNSM-Eiland**, extensively redeveloped islands that now offer innovative housing and superb modern architecture for those looking to make a home just outside the city centre, particularly on the southern peninsulas of **Borneo-Sporenburg**.
SEE ALSO DUTCH DESIGN, P.43

Museums and Music

As with most areas in Amsterdam, the waterfront is home to a selection of top-rate museums. Worth a visit for the building itself, which looks like a ship emerging from the sea, **NEMO** ② is a kids-oriented science museum that attracts some 400,000 visitors every year. The building was designed by the renowned Italian architect Renzo Piano.

Labelled the concert hall of the 21st century, the

Left: the replica of the East Indiaman, the *Amsterdam*.

Architecture

Best explored on foot, the Waterfront throws up a number of interesting architectural sights both new and old. The modern Muziekgebouw vies with NEMO to catch the eye of the tourist, while the glass wave shape of the passenger terminal picks up the nautical theme cleverly. Meanwhile, the **Pakhuis de Zwijger** ⑥, located on Piet Heinkade, offers more traditional architecture, with the old warehouse now a thriving conference and exhibition centre. Head over the water to **Surinamekade** on KNSM-Eiland and as well as enjoying the houseboats and peeking into the artists' studios, you'll also be able to catch a glimpse of the unmistakable **Black Widow tower**. The **Dutch Shell Office**, finally, to the very east of the area, has windows that have been sprinkled with gold dust so that they sparkle in the sunshine.
SEE ALSO ARCHITECTURE, P.29

If your name is Nemo, you can visit NEMO for free! Simply take along proof of identity and you'll receive a free entrance ticket at the ticket office.

Muziekgebouw ③ is a real showpiece on the harbour front. No one musical genre takes centre stage here, with classical, jazz and world music artists all performing regularly. With concerts played every day of the week, take a trip after dark to enjoy the best of the shimmering architecture.

The **National Maritime Museum** *(Nederlands Scheepvaartmuseum)* ④ can be found on Kattenburgerplein, just across the Oosterdok from NEMO. Currently closed for refurbishment with reopening scheduled for 2010, one of the most impressive attractions, namely a replica of the ***Amsterdam*** ⑤, an East Indiaman, is moored and open for tours right next to NEMO.
SEE ALSO ARCHITECTURE, P.28, 29; MUSEUMS AND GALLERIES, P.89; MUSIC, P.91

Right: standout modern architecture at the Muziekgebouw.

De Pijp

A way from the hustle and bustle of central Amsterdam is De Pijp, a city suburb on the up. Just a short tram ride south from Centraal Station, this bohemian district is increasingly finding favour with new residents and visitors, thanks to a spicy melting pot of cultures and nationalities drawn from the old trading routes of the Dutch merchants. As with so much of Amsterdam, the charm of De Pijp is best enjoyed through simply wandering the streets, soaking up the sights, sounds and smells of this multicultural and arty district; a visit to the Albert Cuypmarkt is a great insight into the area's distinctive character.

Heineken Experience

Virtually impossible to miss on the Stadhouderskade, in the northeast corner of the district, the enormous red-brick building housing the **Heineken Experience** ① is a must-visit for beer aficionados, despite the site not seeing commercial brewing for over two decades. Fully renovated for 2009, to make everything all touchy-feely and interactive, this museum traces the 245-year history of the Heineken empire. Among the exhibits is the chance to meet Dr Elion, the inventor of Heineken's magic ingredient, and the opportunity to jump on the Bottle Ride, a moving platform that follows

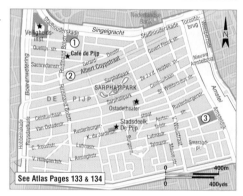

See Atlas Pages 133 & 134

De Pijp was originally built in the 19th century to relive the pressure on the overpopulated Jordaan area. Since then, settlers from numerous different nations, including plenty from the countries that formed part of the Dutch colonial empire, have made it a real multicultural hotspot. Add in to the mix students, artists and young folk looking for afford-able housing and you have an area that's as bohemian as any in Amsterdam.

the production route of a bottle of beer. If all this sounds like thirsty work, fear not: the ticket price includes the reward of a few drinks at the end.

SEE ALSO FOOD AND DRINK, P.56;

Albert Cuypmarkt

The largest concentration of restaurants, bars, cafés, shops and general activity is concentrated in the areas around **Ferdinand Bolstraat**, the thoroughfare linking the **Albert Cuypmarkt** ② with the Heinken Experience. **Café de Pijp** is perhaps the most notable eatery along the strip, due in no small part to the excellent salsa and live music nights served up alongside good food. How-

ever, regardless of your choice of bar, café or restaur-ant, few parts of the city offer better opportunities to mix with locals on their home territory. De Pijp reveals a good deal of Amsterdam's multicultural character, and the choice of eateries on offer reflect this.

For food-lovers, a visit to Amsterdam wouldn't be com-plete without a visit to the thriving Albert Cuypmarkt. The market, which lines the centrally located Albert Cuyp street and its surrounds, began trading in 1904 and now claims over 300 stalls, selling everything from fruit,

Right: shopping at the Albert Cuypmarkt.

Left: De Pijp's narrow streets are packed with cafés and bars.

Much confusion and debate surrounds the origin of the name 'De Pijp'. Some argue it owes its name to the long and narrow nature of the streets, whilst others claim it's all to do with the infamous gas company 'Pipe', that historically supplied energy to the neighbourhood. Either way, people seem to agree that it has nothing to do with the other Dutch use of the word *Pijp*, which is a slang term for male genitalia.

vegetables, cheese, fish and spices to clothes, cosmetics and bedding. Crowded on sunny days and Saturdays, a walk around the eatery-lined market area will yield authentic taste sensations from Surinamese, Moroccan and Syrian restaurants, to Spanish, Indian and Turkish delicatessens. Meanwhile, the area is renowned for offering a typical Amsterdam bar on almost every corner.
SEE ALSO BARS AND CAFÉS, P.35; FOOD AND DRINK, P.55; MARKETS, P.77

Sarphatipark

Regularly rated as one of Amsterdam's top parks, the centrally located **Sarphatipark** is popular with de Pijp's trendy student and young professional set, who make the most of the picturesque setting. The perfect venue for a quick stroll or for picnicking with goodies picked up at the nearby Albert Cuypmarkt, the park has at its heart an elaborate fountain-ringed monument featuring a bronze bust of Amsterdam's city-planner, doctor, philanthropist and all-round local hero, Samuel Sarphati, from whom the park takes its name.
SEE ALSO PARKS AND GARDENS, P.104

Southern Pijp

Amsterdam people themselves will joke that they are interested in anything and everything, with the **NINT Technologie Museum** ③ proof if ever it were needed. Housed in an old diamond-cutting factory on the Tolstraat to the southeast of the district, this is a good rainy-day option for visitors of all ages. The museum focuses on scientific phenomena and their technological applications through interaction and play.
SEE ALSO MUSEUMS AND GALLERIES, P.89

Beyond Amsterdam

With so many sights to see, it's easy to understand why many visitors to Amsterdam never venture beyond the city limits. However, those who do take advantage of the superb public transport network to travel further afield are in for a treat. As well as the classic Dutch windmills, dykes and tulip fields, towns and cities such as Haarlem and Delft offer fabulous architecture, history and world-renowned local products, whilst coastal Noordwijk boasts pristine sand dunes. The famous cheese towns such as Gouda and Aalkmar are also within easy reach, and the eye-opening cut-flower auctions at Aalsmeer offer a fascinating detour en route back to Schiphol Airport.

Volendam ① and Marken ②

Tucked away on the coast of the **Ijselmeer** (Lake Ijsse) a short distance north of Amsterdam, these preserved fishing villages exude charm. The characteristic wooden houses, winding canals and drawbridges combine to create a delightful atmosphere, further enhanced by some excellent restaurants serving exquisite fresh fish straight from the fishing boats. Water-sports fans looking for their fix are well catered for too.

Haarlem ③

As the locals are keen to point out, Haarlem pre-dates Amsterdam by a good few years, dating back to 1245. Thanks to its favourable location on the main trading routes, Haarlem's importance and wealth flourished rapidly, with the architecture and style of the city reflecting this. Over the years nothing has really changed, meaning today it's as charming as ever, with the Dutch almshouses and collection of museums lining the canals of particular note. Haarlem is a shopper's para-

dise too, with a liberal helping of designer boutiques and antique shops to explore. Just 20km (13 miles) from Amsterdam, it's a quick and easy excursion too.

Aalsmeer ④

Covering an area equivalent to around 200 football fields, the home of the **flower auction** at Aalsmeer is listed in the *Guinness Book of Records* as the largest commercial building in the world. Every day, an average of 19 million stems of cut flowers and 2 million plants are unloaded, sold via the reverse auction clocks and reloaded onto trucks for onward delivery in a matter of hours. The informative tour explains how everything works in fascinating detail and gives a guided tour around the premises, where electric carts whiz the blooms around. One for the early birds (the auction takes place between 7–11am), the earlier you get there, the more fun it is. A great calling point if you have a few hours to spare before a flight home from the nearby **Schiphol Airport**.

SEE ALSO TRANSPORT, P.124

Noordwijk ⑤

Besides its spotless beaches, Noordwijk is also known for

Left: William of Orange's mausoleum at Delft's Nieuw Kerk.

on its periphery holding the esteemed position of candle-maker for the Vatican. Museums abound, with cheese (**Museum Gouda**), pharmaceuticals (**Museum De Moriaan**) and Dutch resistance during World War II (**Verzetsmuseum**) all the subject of excellent displays. Gouda is also famous for its ceramic festival and traditional pipes. Situated around an hour's drive south of Amsterdam or around 50 minutes by train, Gouda is a city with a character all of its own.

Delft ⑦

The car-free, compact nature of Delft, coupled with a handy location less than an hour's train ride from Amsterdam, make the city the perfect day-trip destination. A tour round the famous **Delft Blue pottery** is a must, with the Delft Blue tourist train linking the factory with the main city centre places of interest. Those sights include the **Vermeer Centre**, which opened in 2008 to showcase the painter's life and works, and the **Nieuwe Kerk**, housing the mausoleum of the Netherlands' founding father, William of Orange. If you haven't had enough of the canals in Amsterdam, there's another opportunity to get afloat with a tour around the city's medieval centre.

Every year, from late March through to mid May, the **Keukenhof Gardens** near Lisse are transformed into a breathtaking rainbow of colour thanks to around 7 million tulips and other bulb flowers. Such is the scale of the gardens that it holds the title of 'World's Largest Garden'.

Above: a classic Dutch countryside sight.

its bulb flower fields. Located in an area called the **'Dune and Bulb Region'** to the southwest of Amsterdam, the municipality is actually made up of two villages, namely **Noordwijk aan Zee** and **Noordwijk-Binnen**. The former now welcomes nearly 1 million tourists each year, who flock to the area to enjoy the bracing sea air and seaside resort facilities, whilst the latter is all about trade and commerce, with the sand

dunes actually dug out and transformed into bulb fields. Good beachside restaurants are commonplace, as are kite-surfers, with the wide-open spaces simply perfect for one of Holland's fastest-growing leisure activities.

Gouda ⑥

There's more to Gouda than cheese! Whilst the town's fame and fortune have been made in the cheese trade, the town itself is a treasure trove of historic buildings and quirky facts. The weekly **Cheese Market**, held every Thursday in the Market Square, is well worth a visit, as is the imposing **Old City Hall**, completed in 1450. **De Waag**, situated across from the town hall, was built in 1667 as a weigh house for the cheese traders and now survives as a national monument. The **Great St John Church** is famous for its stained-glass windows, with the small candle shop

25

A–Z

In the following section Amsterdam's attractions and services are organised by theme, under alphabetical headings. Items that link to another theme are cross-referenced. All sights that are plotted on the atlas section at the end of the book are given a page number and grid reference.

Architecture

Amsterdam's architectural appeal is very much on a human scale. There are no grand monuments dominating the skyline. Indeed, the best views of Amsterdam are to be had from the tops of church towers which have stood there for centuries. The city has mainly developed to meet the needs of its people, and it's one of the few cities where there is a large population still living right in the centre. Many of its most appealing buildings are private homes, like the tall and gabled canal houses, and one of its most striking buildings is used by tens of thousands of people every day: its railway station.

Centraal Station

Stationsplein; Museum Boat stop 1; Tram: 1, 2, 4, 5, 16, 25; map p.131 C3

In 1876 the Dutch architect Petrus Josephus Hubertus Cuypers was nearing the end of his major Amsterdam project, building the **Rijksmuseum** *(see Museums and Galleries, p.85)*, when an even greater challenge came along. It was to build a new railway station right by the water – in fact, right on the water. It took all his skills to construct three artificial islands, and to drive in some 8,687 wooden stakes, to support the huge structure. It was the biggest engineering project in Amsterdam in the 19th century, and not univer-

sally popular, as it cut the city off from its waterfront. The design echoes Cuypers's work on the Rijksmuseum, combining his own love of neo-Gothic structures with Dutch Renaissance flourishes. Partly because of its location and its function, it is not an immediately attractive building – but it is certainly impressive.
SEE ALSO TRANSPORT, P.124

The Golden Bend (De Gouden Bocht)

Herengracht, between Leidestraat and Vijzelstraat; Tram: 16, 24, 25; map p.133 E2

On a stretch of the Herengracht canal is one of the most graceful sets of buildings in the city, known as the Golden Bend. Rather surprisingly, it was designed not by a notable architect but by the Municipal Carpenter, Hendrik Staets. In the late 16th century the city was becoming overcrowded, with many people fleeing from the Siege of Antwerp and seeking refuge in Amsterdam. The city was

bounded by the Singel canal, beyond which was marshland. Staets proposed building a ring of three more canals, using the earth from digging these as foundations for the buildings in between. With his craftsman's precision, he designed the canals just wide enough for four boats to pass, and each house front was exactly 30m (98ft) wide. They remain as elegant today as ever.

National Maritime Museum (Scheepvaartmuseum)

Kattenburgerplein 1; tel: 020 523 2222; www.scheepvaart museum.nl; closed for refurbishment until mid-2010; Metro: Centraal Station; Bus: 22, 32; map p.134 C1

The Netherlands Maritime Museum (currently closed for a major renovation) is one of the most striking and imposing of the Amsterdam Waterfront buildings. The enormous structure was originally built in the 1650s as a naval store-

Right: NEMO and the *Amsterdam* in the Oosterdok.

Left: the striking Centraal Station building.

Left: gabled houses line the canals.

Gables in Amsterdam are an important feature, being so visible on top of the tall, elegant houses that line the canals. At first simple, they naturally developed as house-holders tried to outdo each other. Single gables gave way to double gables, which had to be functional as well as graceful. In many you will still see the winches that are the only practical way of bringing bulky or heavy items to the top of these narrow-staired houses.

house. This was the Dutch Golden Age, when Amsterdam was the busiest and most important port in the world, and the Dutch East India Company was flourishing. It is architecture as a political statement of a city's importance. The sandstone edifice is supported by 18,000 wooden stakes that were driven into the bed of the River Ij to act as supports, while the four sides conceal a central courtyard where a source of fresh water was kept. This was used to supply the ships that tied up here for supplies and repairs. Normally tied up outside the museum is a replica of an 18th-century East Indiaman sailing ship, the *Amsterdam*, the kind of vessel

that would have been seen here in the building's heyday, and which will be returning from across the dock by NEMO *(see below)* in 2010. SEE ALSO MUSEUMS AND GALLERIES, P.89

NEMO

Oosterdok 2; tel: 020 531 3233; www.e-nemo.nl; Tue–Sun 10am–5pm, daily during school holidays and June–Aug; admission charge; Metro: Centraal Station; map p.131 D4
Even if you know that a kids-oriented science museum isn't your thing, you should still go to take a look at the building. It was designed by Renzo Piano, who also designed the Pompidou Centre in Paris, Potsdammer Platz in Berlin,

the New York Times Building, the Los Angeles County Museum of Art and many other striking modern buildings. He made NEMO to seem like a boat, on Amsterdam's waterfront but about to rise out of the water. On the roof is the highest square in the Netherlands, as the architect wanted to give Amster-dammers a public place in which they could look out over their city, which he felt was lacking elevated points. SEE ALSO MUSEUMS AND GALLERIES, P.89

Pakhuis de Zwijger

Piet Heinkade 179; tel: 020 788 4444; www.dezwijger.nl; Café open Mon–Fri 9am–midnight, other buildings vary with exhibitions and functions; free; Metro: Centraal Station
What was once a dockside warehouse is now a 'warehouse for Media and Culture'. The Pakhuis shows what can be done with these waterfront buildings, as other cities have discovered, and it now houses exhibition and concert halls, TV and radio studios, media centres and the offices of various Amsterdam organisations. And the café is excellent too.

Bars and Cafés

In Amsterdam the borders blur between bars, cafés and other eating and drinking hangouts. If a café serves food beyond the usual cakes and snacks, it might be called an 'Eetcafé', and if it's a traditional old place where the walls have been stained by the smoke of generations (now banned) it will be a 'brown café'. Grand cafés are smarter, with more extensive food menus. See *Coffeeshops, p.40–41*, for information on places that sell cannabis, even though they may also serve regular café snacks and drinks too. For bars that offer live music and dancing, see *Music, p.90–93*, and *Nightlife, p.94–7*.

City Centre

Café de Doelen
Kloveniersburgwal 125; tel: 020 624 9023; Mon–Thur 8am–1am, Fri–Sat 8am–3am; Metro: Waterlooplein; map p.136 B4
The Doelen opened in 1895 and combines a bit of traditional décor with a rough charm that appeals to beer drinkers. It has a decent selection of brews from around the world, and a range of snacks and meals, with its sun terrace that overlooks the canal being popular in summer.

> Brown cafés are a peculiarly Dutch style of place – usually a very old bar/café whose walls have been stained by cigarette smoke and nicotine over the years, as the Dutch are heavy smokers. They will become an endangered species, however, now that the Dutch have followed the example of other countries and banned smoking in public places like bars. People must go outside to smoke, so the days of browning are over.
> See box in Essentials, p.47.

Café Luxembourg
Spui 24; tel: 020 620 6264; www.luxembourg.nl; Sun–Thur 9am–1am, Fri–Sat 9am–2am; Tram: 1, 2, 4; map p.136 A3
There's a very popular terrace outside Amsterdam's answer to a French brasserie-style grand café, while inside is a long bar, banquettes, constant conversation and waiters dashing around serving wines by the glass, coffees, and decent, if pricey, brasserie food.

Hoppe
Spui 18–20; tel: 020 420 4420; www.cafe-hoppe.nl; Sun–Thur 8am–1am, Fri–Sat 8am–2am; Tram: 1, 2, 5; map p.136 A3
No one should visit Amsterdam without at least one drink in the Hoppe, a brown café that dates back to 1670 and claims to serve more beer than anywhere else in the city. There are two parts to the place. The old part's to the right, while to the left is a newer area with seating and music.

De Jaren
Nieuwe Doelenstraat 20–22; tel: 020 625 5771; www.cafe-de-jaren.nl; Sun–Thur 10am–1am, Fri–Sat 10am–2am; Tram: 4, 9, 16; map p.136 B4
The de Jaren only opened in 1990, as a spacious, light and bright place, in contrast to the Dutch tradition for 'cosy' cafés. But the formula worked as it's been busy ever since. Its canalside terrace is always packed, and there's an upstairs dining room that also opens from 5.30pm for dinner.

Wynand Fockink
Pijlsteeg 31; tel: 020 639 2695; www.wynand-fockink.nl; daily 3–9pm; Tram: 4, 9, 16; map p.136 B2
There's been a distillery on this spot since 1679, and it has one of the widest ranges of liqueurs and *jenevers* (Dutch gin, see p.33) in the city. The interior's little changed, with its simple bar and wooden beams, but if you find the choice bewildering just ask for some guidance. If you find one you like, the adjoining shop is open regular shop hours, and there

Right: De Jaren's popular terrace.

Left: the bar at Hoppe, a classic brown café.

restaurant. It's none the worse for that, though, and attracts a sophisticated crowd of drinkers and diners going to the opera as it's part of the Stopera complex of buildings. There's also a large terrace by the Amstel.

In't Aepjen
Zeedijk 1; tel: 020 626 8401; Mon–Thur 3pm–1am, Fri–Sat 3pm–3am; Metro: Centraal Station; map p.131 C4

Built in 1550 near the docks as a hostel and drinking den for sailors, this qualifies as a historic monument as well as one of the absolute best bars of Amsterdam. The wooden exterior (one of only two left in the city) hides a surprisingly bright and pleasant bar inside.

Lime
Zeedijk 104; tel: 020 639 3020; Sun–Thur 5pm–1am, Fri–Sat 5pm–3am; Metro: Nieuwmarkt; map p.137 C1

There are new owners here, so it'll be interesting to see if they can keep Lime's cool reputation (and not just its lime-cool walls) for being a chic place to kick back and enjoy early evening or late night cocktails.

are guided tours of the distillery on Tuesdays and Thursdays from 2–4pm. There is a small fee, but booking is not necessary.

Nieuwmarkt and the Red Light District

Café van Zuylen
Torensteeg 4–8; tel: 020 639 1055; www.cafevanzuylen.nl; Sun–Thur 10am–1am, Fri–Sat 10am–3am; Tram: 13, 14, 17; map p.136 A1

The food and drink menus here are kept pretty simple,

but they're tasty and good value. People come back for the outside terrace (one of the biggest in the city) by the Singel, or to relax and chat in the dark and cosy interior.

Dantzig
Zwanenburgwal 15; tel: 020 620 9039; www.dantzig.info; Mon–Thur 9am–10pm, Fri–Sat 9am–1am, Sun 10am–10pm; Metro: Waterlooplein; map p.136 C4

The Dantzig is done up inside like an old library, but it's all fake – it's a modern café-

Western Canal Belt and the Jordaan

't Arendsnest

Herengracht 90; tel: 020 421 2057; www.arendsnest.nl; Sun–Thur 4pm–midnight, Fri–Sat 4pm–2am; Tram: 1, 2, 5; map p.130 B4

This is an essential stop for the beer-lover, as the 'Eagle's Nest' sells only Dutch beer. If all you know is Heineken, be aware that there are at least 50 other breweries in the Netherlands, and you can find several hundred different brews on the menu here. There are 23 on tap and others are behind the bar, on the bar, in fridges and written on the blackboards at this beer heaven.

Café Chris

Bloemstraat 42; tel: 020 624 5942; www.cafechris.nl; Mon–Thur 3pm–1am, Fri–Sat 3pm–2am, Sun 3–9pm; Tram: 13, 14, 17; map p.130 A4

Look up and check out the gabled roof on this place, which is more bar than café and was built in 1624 when the nearby Westerkerk was also going up. Its builders were the bar's first patrons. Inside there's plenty of light from the windows, a crowded bar, simple tables and chairs, and a general feel that this is how a bar should be.

Finch

Noordermarkt 5; tel: 020 626 2461; Sun–Thur 4pm–1am, Fri–Sat 4pm–3am; Metro: Centraal Station; map p.130 B3

Like the Proust next door (and people often move between them), Finch is a slick bar that attracts a smart crowd. There's a funky feel inside, a décor that's as relaxing as the lounge music usually playing, and in summer you can sit outside on this buzzy square.

Het Molenpad

Prinsengracht 653; tel: 020 625 9680; Sun–Thur noon–1am, Fri–Sat noon–2am; Tram: 1, 2, 5; map p.133 D2

There's a very friendly feel to this neighbourhood place, which has an arty look on the inside thanks to the exhibitions it puts on each month. Outside there's a terrace right by the canal, where you can have a snack or some soup, or something fancier like sea bream with lemon risotto.

't Smalle

Egelentiersgracht 12; tel: 020 623 9617; www.t-smalle.nl; Sun–Thur 10am–1am, Fri–Sat 10am–2am; Tram: 13, 14, 17; map p.130 B4

This used to be a distillery, and the brass, leaded glass

Left: De Vergulde Gaper attracts a local crowd.

Left: relaxing outside trendy Kamer 401.

and chandeliers inside hark back to the golden days, making this one of the more impressive eating and drinking spots in the area. The outside terrace is equally popular as it's in a very attractive canalside spot.

De Vergulde Gaper
Prinsenstraat 30; tel: 020 624 8975; daily 10am–10pm; Tram: 1, 2, 5; map p.130 B3

This used to be a pharmacy, which is why the interior is quaintly decorated with medicinal bottles and old posters. Outside there's a terrace by the Prinsengracht, and inside the snug atmosphere of a classic brown café.

Werck
Prinsengracht 277; tel: 020 627 4079; www.werck.nl; Tue–Thur 3pm–1am, Fri–Sat 3pm–3am; Tram: 13, 17; map p.130 B4

Werck is close to the Anne Frank House and the Westerkerk – in fact it used to be the church's coaching house, though you'd never guess it from the chic, modern and spacious interior, all light woods and bright walls. It's a restaurant/café/bar, and late at night becomes more of a club, so it's hard to categorise but luckily, easy to like.

Southern Canal Belt and Leidseplein

Café Americain
Leidsekade 97; tel: 020 556 3232; www.edenamsterdam americanhotel.com; daily 7am–10pm; Tram: 1, 2, 5; map p.133 D2

Part of the American Hotel, everyone should check in to check out this grand Art Deco café. It's even worth skipping the terrace to enjoy the interior with its stained-glass windows and sense of space. It serves breakfast, lunch, dinner, snacks, or just a coffee or a beer if you only want a quick look.
SEE ALSO HOTELS, P.67

Kamer 401
Marnixstraat 401; tel: 020 620 0614; www.kamer401.nl; Wed–Thur 6pm–1am, Fri–Sat 6pm–3am; Tram: 1, 2, 5; map p.133 D2

The red walls tell you this is a seriously hip place, and it's one of *the* places in the area for pre- and post-dinner drinks. There's no food, but you get DJs playing music as you watch the Amsterdammers watching and being watched.

Weber
Marnixstraat 397; tel: 020 622 9910; www.hotelweber.nl; Sun–Thur 8pm–3am, Fri–Sat 8pm–4am; Tram: 1, 2, 5; map p.133 D2

Part of the Hotel Weber, this is another chic nightspot along the street from the Kamer 401, and attracting a similar crowd of the young and stylish. It's an offbeat place on three levels with Art Deco touches contrasting with animal skins on the walls. It's weird but it works.

Eastern Canal Belt and Rembrandtplein

Café Onder de Ooievaar
Utrechtsestraat 119; tel: 020 624 6836; www.onderde ooievaar.nl; Mon–Thur 10am–1am, Fri–Sat 10am–3am, Sun 10.30am–1am; Tram: 4, 6, 7; map p.134 A3

There's a good range of beers on tap in this unpretentious place, plus seasonal offerings too. Food is no more than things like toasties, omelettes, soup and sandwiches, and there's a timber-beamed bar, a basement pool table and a terrace for when the sun shines. That's pretty much it, but it's all its regulars want.

The Dutch make their own version of gin, called *jenever (pictured, left)*, which comes in several styles and flavours. It was from *jenever* that gin developed, and from which it takes its name. Dutch gin is slightly weaker, and flavoured with such things as herbs and juniper berries. It was originally medicinal, and some drinkers think it still tastes like medicine – but you should try it when in Amsterdam, perhaps at a tasting house like Wynand Fockink *(see p.30)*.

Vooges

Utrechtsestraat 51; tel: 020 330 5670; www.vooges.nl; Sun–Thur 4pm–midnight, Fri–Sat 4pm–3am; Tram: 4, 6, 7; map p.134 A2

At first sight Vooges is nothing special. Some of the wall tiles are crumbling, the chairs look cheap, and the bar isn't the traditional dark polished wood. But it feels lived-in and friendly, and the food and drink menus, though small, have some good choices. And then you find yourself wishing it opened earlier in the day...

The Museum Quarter, Vondelpark and the South

't Blauwe Theehuis

Vondelpark 5; tel: 020 662 0254; www.blauwetheehuis.nl; Sun–Thu 9am–11pm, Fri–Sat 9am–1am; Tram: 1, 2, 6; map p.133 C3

The 1937 Tea House surrounded by the greenery of the Vondelpark is a remarkable building, especially at night when its UFO-like design really does make it seem that the aliens have landed. It's more attractive inside, and though the food and drink are nothing out of the ordinary, it is one of those places you really have to see.

SEE ALSO PARKS AND GARDENS, P.105

Caffe Oslo

Sloterkade 1a; tel: 020 669 9663; www.caffeoslo.nl; Sun–Thur 9am–1am, Fri–Sat 9am–3am; Tram: 1; map p.132 A3

This is a bright and cheerful place, inside and out, the name hinting at the Scandinavian style of the long main room inside. There's a terrace too, and an impressive wine list including a selection of grappas and dessert wines. Lunch options are simple, like baguettes and pastas, but there are more adventurous dishes for dinner.

Jodenbuurt, the Plantage and the Oost

Amstelhaven

Mauritskade 1; tel: 020 665 2672; www.amstelhaven.nl; Sun–Thur 4pm–1am, Fri–Sat 4pm-3am; Metro: Weesperplein; map p.134 B3

The Amstelhaven is where bar merges into club, especially at the weekends when DJs and live bands perform, but mostly it's a huge bar with a terrific big terrace

right alongside the Amstel. The lunch menu is simple and served until 5pm, but at 6pm the dinner menu comes on, with safe but tasty options like rib-eye steak and grilled fish.

Café de Sluyswacht

Jodenbreestraat 1; tel: 020 625 7611; http://sluyswacht.nl; Mon–Thur 11.30am–1am, Fri–Sat 11.30am–3am, Sun 11.30am–7pm; Metro: Waterlooplein; map p.137 C3

One look at the Sluyswacht and you know you're going to like it, a quirky wooden building put up in 1695 as a lock-keeper's cottage. It just looks friendly, and it is, with a cosy interior with a long bar down one side of the room, and outside plenty of tables by the water.

Hesp

Weesperzijde 130–131; tel: 020 665 1202; www.cafehesp.nl; Mon–Thur 10am–1am, Fri–Sat 10am–2am, Sun 11am–1am; Tram: 12

Hesp is typically Amsterdam – part simple café/bar, part restaurant, and a music venue too, with bands playing live on a Sunday afternoon and sometimes other times too. In the evening the lunchtime burgers and sandwiches give way to more adventurous dishes, and there's a decent wine list as well.

The Waterfront

Brouwerij 't Ij

Funenkade 7; tel: 020 320 1786; www.brouwerijhetij.nl; Wed–Sun 3–8pm; Tram: 6, 10; map p.135 D2

In Amsterdam this is where you can actually organise a booze-up in a brewery, as the beer is brewed on the

Above: beer is the local drink of choice.

premises – and it's excellent stuff. There are tours if you want to see how it's done, and the tasting room is nothing fancy, but you can buy a basic snack to soak up the beer and relax for a while. There are some outdoor seats too, and you can't miss the windmill on top.

De Pijp

Biercafé Gollem

Daniel Stalpertstraat 74; tel: 020 676 7117; www.cafegollem.nl; Sun–Thur 4pm–1am, Fri–Sat 2pm–2am; Tram: 16, 24, 25; map p.133 E4

This is a welcome offshoot of the original Gollem in the city centre, the first bar in Amsterdam to serve imported beers. There are over 150 available by the bottle and 14 on tap in this traditional-style bustling bar, handily placed near the Heineken Experience.
SEE ALSO FOOD AND DRINK, P.56

Café de Pijp

Ferdinand Bolstraat 17–19; tel: 020 670 4161; www.goodfood group.nl/pijp.html; Mon–Thur 3.30pm–1am, Fri 3.30pm–3am, Sat noon–2am, Sun noon–1am; Tram: 16, 24, 25; map p.133 E4

This is part of the Good Food Group, which runs an excellent range of bars and

cafés including the **Wildschut** and the **Proust**. Inside it's more café than restaurant, although there's some good food (oysters, entrecôte, vegetarian curries) as well as occasional salsa and live music nights.

Wijnbar Boelen & Boelen

1e van der Helststraat 50; tel: 020 671 2242; www.wijnbar.nl; Tue–Sun 6pm–midnight; Tram: 3, 4, 16; map p.133 E4

There aren't too many really good wine bars in Amsterdam, but this is one of them. There's a good choice of wines by the glass, and plenty by the bottle – even a Netherlands wine. The food is excellent (oysters, scallops, duck breast with calvados), and the interior like a French wine bar crossed with a Dutch bar. An excellent place.

> Bars and cafés vary in both the amount and quality of food they serve. Some offer little more than a toasted sandwich or a bowl of soup, or perhaps even no food at all, but other places might look like rough-and-ready bars yet provide quite delicious proper home-cooked meals. There's no telling in Amsterdam: you just have to try.

Left: a great canalside view from the terrace of the tilting Café de Sluyswacht.

Children

Although the sex 'n' drugs image of Amsterdam means that it's seen very much as an adult destination, it is also extremely child-friendly. You may not wish to wander round the Red Light District ('Daddy, why is that lady only wearing underwear?'), but other than that there's plenty to entertain children – canal cruises, parks, puppet shows, a good zoo, museums and even a special children's restaurant where they can learn how to cook their parents a meal. Regular restaurants mostly welcome children, and are well organised with high chairs and children's portions.

Attractions

Artis Zoo

Plantage Kerklaan 38–40; tel: 020 523 3400; www.artis.nl; daily 9am–6pm, closes 5pm in winter, June–Aug: closes at sunset on Sat; admission charge; Metro Waterlooplein; Tram: 9, 10, 14; map p.135 C2

The Artis is one of the most pleasant city zoos around, and a good way to take kids there is on the **Artis Express**, a special canal boat service that links the zoo with Centraal Station. As well as the animal collection, there's an aquarium, planetarium, two museums and a botanical garden. The zoo dates back to 1838,

The Amsterdam City Council publishes a monthly listings magazine for events in Amsterdam: *Uitkrant*. Although it's in Dutch, it shouldn't be hard to get someone to translate bits of it for you, if you can't speak the language yourself. There's a special children's section called '*Jeugdagenda*'.

but there's a very modern approach to the animals' welfare, which does away with bars and cages. The aquarium has several huge tanks, and includes not only fish like the arowana (which leaps out of the water to catch spiders and insects), but the secrets of what lies beneath the surface of Amsterdam's canals. Not cheap, but a good day out.

Tropenmuseum Junior

Tropenmuseum, Linnaeusstraat 2; tel: 020 568 8233; www.tropenmuseumjunior.nl; daily 10am–5pm; admission charge, free for under-5s; Tram: 9, 14; map p.135 D3

Inside Amsterdam's lovely Tropenmuseum (Tropical Museum) is a special junior version aimed at children from 6–12. It has changing exhibitions which aim both to entertain and to educate children about life in tropical countries, always in a stimulating and fun fashion. There are music and dance performances, where the language barrier is seldom a problem, and plenty of interactive exhibits too.

SEE ALSO MUSEUMS AND GALLERIES, P.88

TunFun

Mr Visserplein 7; tel: 020 689 4300; www.tunfun.nl; daily 10am–6pm; admission charge;

Left: visit the animals at the Artis Zoo in the Plantage.

Left: there is boundless fun for kids at TunFun.

This café that's run by children is a quirky and unique idea that you somehow find only in Amsterdam. During the week you can just walk in, and if you're in the city with children you should definitely have a meal, or at least a coffee, here. On some weekends there are cookery classes which have to be booked ahead, with the children occupied during the day preparing the meals, and learning to serve too.

Shopping

De Beestenwinkel
Staalstraat 11; tel: 020 623 1805; www.beestenwinkel.nl; Mon noon–6pm, Tue–Fri 10am–6pm, Sat 10am–5.30pm, Sun noon–5.30pm; Tram: 9, 14; map p.136 C4
This delightful toy shop is where your children are likely to find a souvenir of their visit to Amsterdam, from the wide range of stuffed animals, wooden toys, ceramic chickens and other fun stuff, with special sections for babies' toys and games too. There's another branch at: Ijburglaan; tel: 020 567 569; Tue–Fri 9am–6pm, Sat 9am–5pm

't Klompenhuisje
Nieuwe Hoogstraat 9a; tel: 020 622 8100; www.klompen huisje.nl; Mon–Sat 10am–6pm; Tram: 9, 14; map p.136 C3
Amsterdam is renowned for its array of specialist shops, which are often attractions in their own right. If you want a real Dutch souvenir for your children, this shoe shop caters exclusively for little feet and makes it an enjoyable experience to shop for a pair of wooden clogs, wellingtons, slippers and shoes, some with quite amazing designs.

Right: traditional clogs for sale at 't Klompenhuis.

Metro: Waterlooplein; Tram: 9, 14; map p.137 D4
What was a dreary traffic underpass has been transformed into an underground playground for children from ages 1–12. There are slides, trampolines, pools, a football pitch, jump cushions, bowling and occasional discos and parties. Children must have an adult with them, and there's a café to relax in too.

Babysitting Services

Oppascentrale Kriterion
Timorplein 24–26; tel: 020 624 5848; www.kriterionoppas.org; Mon 9am–11pm, Tue–Sun 4.30–8pm; admission charge; transport details; map p.135 E2
This non-profit organisation is available through a yearly membership fee and was founded in 1946 by students who had been part of the Resistance movement during World War II. Fees go towards helping students pay for their studies. Further information is on their very good website in Dutch and English.

Essentials
For children's supplies, nappies and formula milk etc, look for the bigger branches of the most common supermarket chains like **Albert Heijn** and **HEMA**, or the big department stores such as **De Bijenkorf** on Dam Square.
SEE ALSO FOOD AND DRINK, P.56; SHOPPING, P.115

Restaurant

Kinderkookkafé
Vondelpark 6b/Overtoom 325; tel: 020 625 3257; www.kinder kookkafe.nl; Mon–Fri 9am–5pm, check website for weekend cookery lessons; Tram: 1; map p.132 B3

37

Churches and Synagogues

The skyline of central Amsterdam has not been taken over by high-rise buildings, as many city centres have. As a result, the towers of its churches *(kerks)* are still prominent, as intended when they were built. Those with towers that are open to the public also offer some of the best views over the city, if you can manage to climb them. As in many of the city's hotels, there are no lifts and the stairs are long and steep. The effort is worth it though. The churches themselves are among the oldest and grandest buildings in the city.

City Centre

Engelse Kerk

Begijnhof 48; tel: 020 624 9665 (for concert ticket information only); daily, hours vary, Sun service 10.30am; free; Tram: 1, 2, 4; map p.136 A3

The English Reformed Church occupies a prominent part of the Begijnhof *(see p.98)*, where there has been a chapel since 1397. The present building was completed in 1492, though the church fell into disrepair in the 16th century. In 1607 it was given to a congregation of English-speaking worshippers who were petitioning the town hall for a place of worship. They were given this building, and a programme of restoration began. In the 18th century links were made with the Scottish Church too, and today the Engelse Kerk is an active place of worship for the English and Scottish ex-pat communities.

Nieuwe Kerk

Dam Square; tel: 020 638 6909; www.nieuwekerk.nl; daily 10am–6pm, Thur until 10pm; admission charge; Tram: 1, 2, 4; map p.136 A1

The Nieuwe Kerk is on Dam Square, across from the Royal Palace, and has an unusual dual role. It is one of the most prominent churches in the Netherlands, where heads of state are crowned, where royal marriages often take place, and where the annual Remembrance Day service take place each 4 May. Most visitors, though, will primarily see it as an exhibition space, as there is an ongoing exhibition programme.

The 'new' church dates from 1408, and its name distinguishes it from the city's 'old' Oude Kerk *(see below)*. It was damaged by the serious fires which ravaged the city in the 15th century, and again by the Great Fire in 1645. To uncover a fuller history of this fascinating building, you can organise a personal guided tour, which has to be booked in advance and is available in several languages.

Nieuwmarkt and the Red Light District

Oude Kerk

Oudekerksplein 1; tel: 020 625 8284; www.oudekerk.nl; Mon–Sat 11am–5pm, Sun 1–5pm; admission charge; Tram: 4, 9, 16; map p.136 C1

The 'Old Church' is indeed the

The **Nieuwe Kerk** *(pictured, right)* in the city of Delft is a must-see if you are taking a day trip to the home of the famous Delft Blue pottery. It is the resting place of the Netherlands' founder, William of Orange, but is also notable for its stunning stained-glass windows. It took 15 years to build and was completed in 1396. *See Beyond Amsterdam, p.25.*

Left: the stained-glass windows at the Oude Kerk.

There are few synagogues in the city today, as the Jewish community was of course virtually wiped out during the Nazi occupation of World War II. Some synagogues, like the Sephardic Synagogue that was dedicated in 1675, were vandalised during the war, and although later restored, they no longer have big enough congregations to support their upkeep.

oldest in the city, built on a mound near the Amstel where previously a wooden chapel had been built in 1306. The present church is thought to have been the city's first parish church and dates back to the late 13th or early 14th century. Amsterdam was growing so quickly that within 30 years the church was too small, so there then followed an almost constant sequence of expansions. The church was damaged in the city fires of 1421 and 1452, but by the mid-1500s had 38 separate altars. Today it is used as an exhibition space.

The Western Canal Belt and the Jordaan

Noordekerk
Noordermarkt 48; tel: 020 624 7819; www.noorderkerk.org; Mon, Wed 10.30am–3pm, Thur, Sat 11am–1pm, Sun 1.30–5.30pm; free; Bus: 18, 22; map p.130 B3

The 'Northern Church' was built here at the busy Noordermarkt market place in the 1620s, as the city centre population began to spread out and occupy the Jordaan

Above: the bell in the Westerkerk tower.

district. It is a rather severe-looking church, but still has a very active congregation and it was renovated in 1997–8. There are two Sunday services, at 10am and 7pm, and also regular concerts (www.noorderkerkconcerten.nl).

Westerkerk
Prinsengracht 277–279; tel: 020 624 7766 (tower information: 020 689 2565); www.westerkerk.nl; Apr–Sept Mon–Fri 11am–3pm; admission charge to tower; Tram: 13, 14, 17; map p.130 B4

The Westerkerk was opened to its first worshippers on Whit Sunday in 1631, and has been an important city landmark ever since. Rembrandt was buried here in 1669, and

although no one knows where, there is a plaque inside that is close to the likely spot. It was the tower of the Westerkerk that Anne Frank could see from her house, and which she recorded in her diary. At 85m (278ft) high, the tower does give one of the best views over the city, but it is only open in summer. Visitors should phone for the tower's opening times.

Jodenbuurt, the Plantage and the Oost

Portuguese-Israelite Synagogue
Mr Visserplein 3; tel: 020 624 5351 (tour information: 020 531 0380); Sun–Fri 10am–4pm (Nov–Mar: closes 2pm on Fri); admission charge; Metro: Waterlooplein; map p.137 D4

Also known just as the Portuguese Synagogue or the Esnoga (which means Synagogue in the Judaeo-Spanish language of Ladino), it was opened in 1675 and is one of the largest synagogues in the world. Like many city buildings it rests on wooden piles, but in the Esnoga these can be visited by taking a boat onto the water underneath. The synagogue is open to visitors, but guided tours must be arranged in advance.

Coffeeshops

A
msterdam's famed coffeeshops are the *raison d'être* for some visitors' trip to the city. These generally function as regular cafés, but with the added twist of being licensed to sell cannabis too, even though smoking weed is still (contrary to what most people think) illegal in the Netherlands. It is simply tolerated. The laws are quite strict and have been getting stricter *(see below)*, and the July 2008 smoking ban in the Netherlands has further complicated the issue. There's also been a restriction on the number of new licences being handed out, but there are still an estimated 150 or so coffeeshops in the city.

Smoking in Amsterdam

On 1 July 2008 the Netherlands joined the growing band of countries which banned smoking in public places, including restaurants and cafés. This initially presented a problem for the city's renowned coffeeshops, whose main business is allowing the smoking of cannabis on the premises, but in fact, the law governs the smoking of tobacco, nothing else. Separate rooms are required for anyone smoking a mix of tobacco and cannabis, but if tobacco is not involved then strictly

Many coffeeshops sell things like muffins, cakes and brownies with cannabis in them, sometimes under the generic name of 'space cakes'. They're more expensive than regular cakes, so there's little chance of you ordering one unintentionally. They can be as strong as smoking a cigarette, but take longer to have an effect. If in any doubt at all, don't be afraid to ask one of the staff for advice.

speaking it can still be smoked in a public place. However, coffeeshop owners have reacted in different ways to the ban, and some have introduced completely separate smoking rooms. Others have simply defied the ban and carried on as before. It still remains to be seen what will happen to them.

The difficulty lies in the fact that smoking cannabis is illegal, but has been tolerated for many years. Provided it harms no one, the police look the other way. In recent years there has been concern that the coffeeshops, along with the Red Light District, have been bad for the city's image and are having a detrimental effect on the lives of the citizens, so the police have started to become less tolerant.

At the moment it is still fine to smoke cannabis in a licensed coffeeshop, and to buy up to 5 grams a day for your personal consumption. You must be 18, and may be asked to produce ID, such as a passport or driving licence. Under-18s are not admitted,

Above: a bowl of the goods on display at Barney's Coffeeshop.

and you cannot bring your own drugs onto the premises. You also cannot carry more than 5 grams with you. Follow these guidelines, and whatever the coffeeshop says, and you will be fine. The majority of coffeeshops are in the city centre and in the Jordaan area.

SEE ALSO ESSENTIALS, P.47

City Centre

Abraxas
Jonge Roelensteeg 12; tel: 020 489 1933; www.abraxas paradise.nl; daily 10am–1am; Tram: 13, 14, 17; map p.136 A2
If you want to surf and smoke,

Left: the laid-back environs of La Tertulia.

ure. There are three different levels, though it's still a small place and often full.

Western Canal Belt and the Jordaan

Siberie
Brouwersgracht 111; tel: 020 623 5909; www.coffeeshopsiberie.nl; Sun–Thur 11am–11pm, Fri–Sat 11am–midnight; Metro: Centraal Station; map p.130 B3
There are art displays and chess to play in this very laid-back café, where there's often something going on – DJs, poetry readings, astrology readings. It's on the edge of the Jordaan, a short stroll from Centraal Station, and the kind of place which, if you find it early on in your visit, can become a regular hang-out.

La Tertulia
Prinsengracht 312; www.coffeeshopamsterdam.com; Tue–Sat 11am–7pm; Tram: 13, 14, 17; map p.133 D1
Look for the mural of Vincent van Gogh on the wall outside this place, whose name is the Spanish word for a social gathering, so there's definitely a Mediterranean vibe here. Inside there's a collection of crystals and a range of snacks and regular drinks, and seating outside by the Prinsengracht canal.

or play chess while sipping a hash-infused hot chocolate, the long-established Abraxas is the place to be. Even without the main attraction, and the cakes, muffins and shakes you can also get, it's a nice, relaxed City Centre café.

Barney's Coffeshop
Haarlemmerstraat 98; tel: 020 625 9761; www.barneys-amsterdam.com; daily 7am–10pm; Metro: Centraal Station; map p.130 B3
Another of the most famous Amsterdam coffeeshops, that's been in business since 1986 and now has several outlets around the city, several on the same street, though only this coffeeshop has a licence to sell cannabis.

De Dampkring
Handboogstraat 29; tel: 020 638 0705; www.dampkring.nl; daily 10am–1am; Tram: 1, 2, 5; map p.136 A4
One of the most famous coffeeshops in the city, which has been in business since 1993 and features in the 2004 Brad Pitt movie *Ocean's Twelve*. It's won the Hightimes Cannabis Cup award several times – the Amsterdam coffeeshop equivalent of gaining your Michelin star. It's also got a big range of merchandise, for that special souvenir.

Kadinsky
Rosmarijnsteeg 9; tel: 020 624 7023; Sun–Thur 10am–1am, Fri–Sat 10am–2am; Tram: 1, 2, 5; map p.136 A3
Famous for its chocolate-chip cookies, this is the most famous of several Kadinsky coffeeshops around the city, and also noted for its computerised weighing scales for an absolutely accurate meas-

Right: De Dampkring is renowned and always busy.

Dutch Design

The Dutch do things differently. Although it's hard to say why that is, or to define what it is, they always seem to be able to look at the world from a slightly different angle. This applies to style and design as much as anything else. Rotterdam is the city where you will see contemporary Dutch design applied to the landscape, whereas in the old city of Amsterdam it isn't quite as easy to do that. However, there are some bold new buildings (*see Architecture, p.28–9*) and plenty of shops around town where you can find – and buy – the kind of design objects you simply don't see elsewhere.

Design Shopping

Droog Design
Staalstraat 7a/b; tel: 020 523 5050; www.droog.com; Tue–Sat noon–6pm; Tram: 4, 9, 14; map p.136 B4
The Droog Design group is a design collective, now based in Amsterdam, whose work has become internationally famous and has been honoured with exhibitions in style-conscious cities like Barcelona, Milan and New York. Their furniture manages to be both eye-catching and comfortable, and one of their most famous works is a chest of drawers where the drawers are all different, and piled on top of each other in an artfully random way, showing how conventional most furniture design has been.

Frozen Fountain
Prinsengracht 645; tel: 020 622 9375; www.frozenfountain.nl; Mon 1–6pm, Tue–Fri 10am–6pm, Sat 10am–5pm; Tram: 1, 2, 5; map p.133 D2
The Frozen Fountain shop has been in business since 1985 and sells furniture, fabrics and other home acces-

sories, and carries the work of many young Dutch designers as well as international names. Featured artists/designers include Claudy Jongstra, who works in felt and has exhibited worldwide, and the well-known Dutch furniture designer Piet Hein Eek, whose work in materials including scrap metal and leftover timber really has to be seen to be believed. You can also commission the artists to create unique works for you.

Galerie Binnen
Keizersgracht 82; tel: 020 625 9603; Wed–Sat noon–6pm; Tram: 1, 3, 5; map p.130 B3
This is a gallery not for painting or sculpture but for domestic, interior and industrial designs. After each exhibition, which can be on themes as varied as tables and chairs or ceramics, any unsold items may go into the permanent collection, and be available for later pur-

chase. It's a good place to combine browsing with possible shopping.

SML.X
Donker Curtiusstraat 11; tel: 020 681 2837; www.smlx.com; Mon, Fri 10am–6pm; Tram: 10
'Not just a t-shirt...' is the boast of this place, and you know you're dealing with artists when the shop only opens two days a week. The t-shirts are created by a wide range of local artists, from graphic designers and painters to graffiti artists, who do their own thing and then

Right: reinventions of furniture and eye-catching homewares at Droog Design.

Left: quirky home design at Frozen Fountain.

One of the best places to see examples of modern Dutch design is in the architecture of the dockland area that was developed in the 1990s and is known as **Borneo Sporenburg**. It is to the east of the City Centre and comprises two islands, Borneo and Sporenburg. This area shows off some startling modern buildings, including three housing developments: **The Whale**, **Fountainhead** and the **Ij Tower**.

sell them in the shop. The results are usually stunning, and they also do long-sleeved shirts and polo shirts, for men, women and children. Quite often, the kids get the best designs.

SPRMRKT
Rozengracht 191–193; tel: 020 330 5601; www.sprmrkt.nl; Sun–Mon noon–6pm, Tue–Sat 10am–6pm, Thur until 8pm; Tram: 13, 14, 17; map p.130 A4
The warehouse-size store of SPRMRKT focuses on furniture and includes modern designers working in retro-style as well as some original stuff, like 1950s furniture that's so kitsch it's now classic. They've also been expanding into clothes and stock original 1970s shirts in among the shoes and jewellery. There's sometimes live music at the weekends, as well as exhibitions and other events, and the shop is also a great place to buy books on Dutch design.

Institutes

ARCAM
Prins Hendrikkade 600; tel: 020 620 4878; www.arcam.nl; Tue–Sat 1–5pm; Metro: Waterlooplein; map p.134 C1
The Amsterdam Centre for Architecture was built in 1986 but still manages to look contemporary, if not futuristic, with its swirling style, set by the water. It is an information centre for the city's architecture – both modern and historic – as well as a venue for exhibitions and talks, and organises fascinating architectural tours of Amsterdam. There are also books on design and architecture for sale, and architectural maps of Amsterdam.

Environment

The environment is an important concern for the Dutch. The geography of the country and the social thinking of its people have forced issues such as rising sea levels, wind energy and globalisation high up the political agenda. While the Netherlands is known for its windmills, bicycles and free thinking, the statistics behind the image are compelling. Over 60 percent of the country lies below sea level, making it vulnerable to flooding. And as the world's third-largest exporter of agricultural produce, supporting a highly urbanised and densely populated nation, it's no wonder that sustainability has become an obsession.

Emissions Record

The Netherlands has one of the highest levels of industrial carbon dioxide emissions per capita in the world. Efforts at controlling air pollution have made worthwhile progress, though as yet, conversion to the use of renewable energy is happening relatively slowly. A league table of European Countries compiled by the EU in 2008 placed the Netherlands third from bottom, with only 2.4 percent of its energy deriving from renewable sources (by contrast, Sweden is at the top of the table by already running at 40 percent).

Flood Protection

The Netherlands has long been alert to the dangers of rising sea levels. In the past, Holland's precious agricultural plains were kept cultivable by a host of windmills pumping water into a network of dykes. Since the 1950s, however, when a storm surge broke through sea defences causing devastation and the loss of 1,800 lives, a more reliable and

Of animal species found in the Netherlands, six mammal species and three bird species are threatened with extinction. Those endangered include the Atlantic sturgeon, the Atlantic ridley turtle, the slender-billed curlew and Spengler's freshwater mussel.

comprehensive solution has been sought. Indeed, by law, flood defences are now required to provide a 1-in-10,000-years level of protection. New Orleans, by comparison, had only 1-in-100-years protection.

The answer to this problem is known as the **Delta Works**. Its main strategy is to shorten the Dutch coastline by damming the mouths of several estuaries and thus reducing the number of dykes that need to be raised. Even so, when it was completed in 1997 after almost 50 years, it had entailed the building of 10,250 miles (16,500km) of dykes and 300 dams and other structures.

Sadly, against rising sea levels, the Delta Works are

now deemed to be inadequate, and a new phase of engineering works has begun. Over 250 miles (400km) of dykes will be reinforced by 2015, and the government is even considering upgrading flood protection to a 1-in-100,000-years level at an annual cost of 0.2 percent of the country's GDP.

Travel and Carbon Offsetting

The carbon footprint of an aeroplane journey is significantly larger than that of many other forms of motorised transport, since the impact of releasing greenhouse gases at high altitudes is far more harmful. A single person's share of the emissions associated with a return flight between California and Europe, for example, amounts to approximately 2.5 tonnes of carbon dioxide – equivalent to the annual output of the average car.

While many journeys from

Right: Amsterdam requires strong defences to prevent the city's canals from flooding.

Left: getting around by bike is a way of life for locals.

duced by your particular flight.
SEE ALSO TRANSPORT, P.124

Cycling

The Dutch are renowned for their environmentally sound allegiance to two wheels rather than four, purchasing approximately 1.5 million bicycles each year. You can join them for a day by hiring a bike at **Bike City** (Bloemgracht 68–70; tel: 020 626 3721; www.bikecity.nl), **Mac Bike** (Centraal Station, Stationsplein 12; 020 620 0985; www.macbike.nl) or **Rent-A-Bike** (Damstraat 20–2; tel: 020 625 5029; www.bikes.nl).
SEE ALSO TRANSPORT, P.125; WALKS, BIKE RIDES AND CANAL TOURS, P.126

outside Europe to Amsterdam cannot help but be by plane, visitors to the country can help reduce the environmental effect of their visit by offsetting the emissions associated with their means of transport. Travellers can offset their share of the carbon footprint by purchasing carbon credits according the distance travelled. The credits are then invested in renewable energy and energy-efficiency programmes in developing countries.

Carbon credits can be purchased through offset schemes such as www.climatecare.org and www.carbonneutral.com. These websites have simple calculators that allow you to work out your share of the several tonnes of carbon dioxide pro-

Environmental Organisations

GreenLeft (GroenLinks)
Tel: 070 318 3030;
www.groenlinks.nl
The Dutch Green Party.
See also DWARS (www.dwars.org), the independent youth wing of the party.

Milieu Defensie
Nieuwe Looiersstraat 31;
tel: 020 6262 620;
www.milieudefensie.nl
The Dutch branch of Friends of the Earth.

Samenwerkingsverband Nationale Parken
Willem Witsenplein 6, The Hague; www.nationaalpark.nl
The organisation administering the country's 20 national parks.

SOVON – Dutch Centre for Field Ornithology
Rijksstraatweg 178, Beek-Ubbergen; tel: 024 684 8111;
www.sovon.nl
They have a useful website for bird-spotters, with a section in English listing all bird species found in the country, together with their distributions and populations.

Essentials

A s one of the world's most liberal, easygoing cities, visitors to Amsterdam shouldn't find anything to detract from their enjoyment of this cosmopolitan metropolis. Convenient opening hours abound, crime is no worse than in any other major city and tourists are well catered for, with detailed information always available in numerous different languages. The city's residents are friendly and always willing to offer helpful advice and, as is typical of most Western European cities, standards of service and quality are high, with everything designed to help those in Amsterdam enjoy their favourite pastime, having a good time.

Business Hours

Normal shopping hours are 9am–6pm (5pm on Saturday). Late-night shopping is on Thursday until 9pm. Most shops open noon–5pm on Sunday. All shops close for one half-day a week, usually Monday, when they open 1–6pm. Some supermarkets remain open until at least 7pm on week nights. Many grocery stores, such as the **Albert Heijn** chain, are open most evenings until 10pm. Businesses operate Mon–Fri 8.30am–5pm, whilst banks open weekdays 9am–4pm. SEE ALSO FOOD AND DRINK, P.56; SHOPPING, P.117

Climate

The Netherlands has a temperate climate, making extremes rare. Amsterdam's average winter daytime temperatures are around 5°C (41°F), falling to 1°C (34°F) at night, although temperatures can plummet to −10°C (14°F). The summer average is 22°C (72°F), falling to around 13°C (55°F) at night. In the occasional heatwaves, temperatures can rise to 30°C (86°F).

Rain occurs year-round, but spring is generally the driest time and ideal for tulip enthusiasts.

Crime and Safety

Amsterdam is a centre of the drugs trade; although you are unlikely to be affected by big-time drugs-related crime, take precautions against becoming a victim of pickpocketing and bag-snatching, and of the less common but more serious violent robberies. Watch wallets and bags, especially at busy transport hubs. Exercise caution in certain areas after dark: the Red Light District's narrow alleyways, deserted canalsides and Vondelpark. Never photograph women in the Red Light District.

There are police stations around the city, with police headquarters for non-urgent matters at: 117 Elandsgracht, tel: 0900 8844; map p.133 D1

Customs

Personal possessions are not liable to duty and tax provided you are staying for less than

| Emergency Numbers |
| For Police, Fire, Ambulance: dial 112. |

six months. There is no restriction on the amount of currency that you can import, but prohibited or restricted goods include plants, flowers, weapons and recreational drugs. For travel within the EU, the following goods restrictions apply: 800 cigarettes, 400 cigarillos, 200 cigars or 1kg tobacco, 10l spirits over 22%, 20l alcohol less than 22%, 90l wine (no more than 60l sparkling wine) or 110l beer, 50g perfume and 250ml eau de toilette.

Non-EU citizens are limited to smaller amounts.

Disabled Travellers

The Royal Association for Disability and Rehabilitation (RADAR) in the UK has information on planning holidays, equipment for rent and accommodation. Its address is:

12 City Forum, 250 City Rd, London EC1V 8AF, tel: (020) 7250 3222.

Left: catching up on emails at an internet café *(see p.48)*.

as they are often fake or cut with rat poison.
SEE ALSO COFFEESHOPS, P.40

Electricity

The standard for electricity is 230 volts AC and therefore a two-pin European model adaptor plug is needed. Hotels may have a 110- or 120-volt outlet for shavers.

Embassies and Consulates

CONSULATES IN AMSTERDAM:
British Consulate: 44 Koningslaan; tel: 020 676 4343
Consulate General of the US: American Citizens Services; 19 Museumplein; tel: 020 575 5309

EMBASSIES IN THE HAGUE
Australian Embassy: 4 Carnegielaan, 2517 KH; tel: 070 310 8200
Embassy of Ireland: 9 Dr Kuyperstraat, 2514 BA; tel: 070 363 0993
New Zealand Embassy: Eisenhowerlaan 77N, 2517 KK; tel: 070 346 9324
These offices are generally open 8.30am–4.30pm (some only in the morning) and are

Most major museums and galleries have wheelchair access, although Amsterdam's cobbled streets and narrow staircases are not ideal. The **Stichting Gehandicapten Overleg Amsterdam** provides a downloadable (in Dutch) Accessibility Guide and (in English) Public Transport Access guide on its website www.sgoa.nl, tel: 020 577 7955. A new website informing visitors of public buildings' and attractions' accessibility will be launched early in 2009.

Drugs

It is permitted to smoke cannabis or hashish (but not regular tobacco) in licensed 'coffeeshops' in Amsterdam. These establishments can sell a maximum of 5 grams to customers over the age of 18, and the possession of this, although technically against the law, is tolerated by the authorities. However, the smell of a joint is not appreciated in other bars. Buying hard drugs or soft drugs on the street is strictly illegal and can be dangerous

Below: posters remind punters of the new smoking laws.

VANAF 1 JULI IS DE HORECA ROOKVRIJ.

Strange as it may seem given the Netherlands' famously relaxed attitude to smoking marijuana, smoking tobacco in public areas such as bars and restaurants has been prohibited since July 2008, in line with European Union law. This means that while it is still legal to smoke a pure-cannabis joint indoors, it can't be mixed with tobacco. If someone wants to roll their joint with tobacco, then they have to smoke it outside. *See also Coffeeshops, p.40.*

regular cafés are offering wireless internet, some free of charge.

easyInternet café
33 Damrak; daily 9am–10pm; map p.136 B1

Underworld C@fé
7a Voetboogstraat; tel: 638 1388; daily noon–10pm; map p.136 A4

Media

The main national newspapers are *NRC Handelsblad*, the most respected paper, the more left-wing *De Volkskrant*, *De Telegraaf* on the political right, and the Protestant *Trouw*. The monthly English-language *Amsterdam Day by Day* gives listings and reviews of events, available from VVV offices and newspaper kiosks. *Amsterdam Weekly* is an English-language city paper, containing listings, insightful articles and restaurant reviews.

The *Uitkrant*, available at the Uitburo ticket shop on the Leidseplein, is a free monthly publication which, although in Dutch, is easily readable for concert venues and performance dates. For events reservations: tel: 0900 0191.

Money

ATMS

The city's automatic cash-dispensers can be accessed by foreign credit cards or cash cards with the Cirrus or Plus logo. ATMs are found all over the city.

CHANGING MONEY

Bureaux de change are located at post offices and national banks (at good rates); beware high commission rates at hotels. Check www.xe.com for current exchange rates.

closed on their countries' and Dutch public holidays.

Health and Medical Care

European Union citizens require a **European Health Insurance Card (EHIC)** to obtain free emergency medical treatment; this is not a substitute for insurance and doesn't cover non-urgent or ongoing treatment. It is advisable to obtain medical travel insurance before travelling in all cases.

HOSPITALS AND CLINICS
Tourist Doctor
112 Bloemgracht; tel: 020 427 5011/062 723 5380; map p.130 A4
Provides a GP service as well as hotel visits and telephone consultations.

Onze Lieve Vrouwe Gasthuis
9 Oosterpark; tel: 020 599 9111
Amsterdam's most central hospital. Has an outpatients department and an emergency casualty ward.

Academisch Medisch Centrum (AMC)
9 Meibergdreef; tel: 020 566 9111
The city's main hospital. Has an outpatients department and an emergency casualty ward.

MEDICAL ADVICE
Central Doctors Service (Centrale Doktersdienst)
tel: 0900 592 3434
Provides 24-hour emergency referrals for appropriate medical and dental care.

PHARMACIES
Pharmacies *(apotheken)* are normally open Mon–Fri 8.30am–5.30pm. Weekend and late-night pharmacies operate on a rotating basis. A list of out-of-hours pharmacies is posted on the front door of every *apotheek*.

Internet

Some internet cafés have scanners and colour printers. An increasing number of

The **Grenswisselkantoren NV (GWK)** (Stationsplein; Mon–Sat 8am–10pm, Sun 9am–10pm; map p.131 C3) is a national financial institution where you can exchange any currency and use credit cards or travellers' cheques.

CURRENCY

The euro (€) is the Netherlands' currency unit, which is divided into 100 cents. Euro notes come in denominations of 5, 10, 20, 50, 100, 200 and 500; coins are 1, 2, 5, 10, 20 and 50 cents, as well as €1 and €2. Major hotels, restaurants and shops accept all major credit cards, although smaller businesses may not.

TIPPING

Service is almost always included but tipping between 5–10 percent is acceptable in restaurants and when paying for taxis.

Postal Services

Most post offices are open weekdays 9am–5pm; the main branch at Singel 250–6 also opens 10am–1.30pm on Saturdays. Stamps are available from post offices and some newsstands.

Main post offices provide poste restante facilities, but you need a passport to collect your mail. You can also send a fax, make long-distance calls (after buying a telephone card) and make photocopies.

Telephones

Most telephone boxes take phonecards which are available from post offices and large stores; some take coins and credit cards. When dialling an Amsterdam number from outside the city, use

the area code **020**. To dial an Amsterdam number from a public phone inside the city, you do not need to use the code, just dial the 7-digit number.

Remember that if you are calling a local number from your mobile phone it is necessary to dial **0031** (for the Netherlands) followed by the code for Amsterdam (**20**), because you are still operating through your home service provider. Numbers beginning with 0900 are charged at a higher rate, while 0800 numbers are toll-free. Call **0800 0410** for operator assistance.

Toilets

Public toilets in Amsterdam are few and far between, and the very public men's urinals are pretty grim, if innovative. However, in cafés and fast-food restaurants you can use the toilet either free or for a charge of 25–50 cents.

Tourist Information

Amsterdam Tourist Board (VVV)
10 Stationsplein, tel: 0900 400 4040; www.amsterdamtourist.nl; open Mon–Fri 9am–6pm, Sat–Sun 10am–6pm; map p.131 C3
The main tourist office is opposite **Centraal Station**. There is also an office inside the station (Platform 2; daily 9am–7pm). There are alternative VVV bureaus at the locations below. All offices

have the same telephone number:
1 Stadhouderskade; daily 9am–5pm; map p.133 D2
8 Paulus Potterstraat; daily 8.30am–5pm; map p.133 D3.
Schipol Airport
A tourist information office at **Arrivals 2** (daily 7am–10pm) is useful for booking accommodation.

Visas

Visitors from the European Union, the US, Canada, Australia, New Zealand and most other European countries require only a valid passport. Citizens of most other countries must obtain a visa in advance from Dutch embassies or consulates in their home countries.

Websites

www.amsterdamtourist.nl
The Amsterdam Tourist Board's comprehensive website is recommended.
www.holland.com
For a wider vista on Holland, the Netherlands Board of Tourism's site is useful.
www.amsterdamhotspots.nl
A good, independent site which covers the hottest places for eating, smoking (hash), dancing and more.
www.dinner-in-amsterdam.nl
Another helpful independent site, specialising in restaurant reviews.

Right: the public men's urinals.

Festivals and Events

Whether it's football, art, religion, sex, beer, bicycles or windmills, the Dutch will set a time aside to celebrate it. And Amsterdam's civic values, open squares and grassy parks provide the ideal environment for gatherings of all kinds. The calendar below covers the main events, but it may also be worth consulting the city's tourist office for up-to-the-minute information *(see Essentials, p.49)*. For further specialised festivals and events, see *Film, p.52*, *Gay and Lesbian, p.61*, *Literature, p.74*, and *Theatre and Dance, p.122.*

Public Holidays
1 Jan – New Year's Day
Good Friday, Easter Sunday and Monday
30 April – Queen's Day
4 May – Remembrance Day
5 May – Liberation Day
Ascension Day
Whit Sunday and Monday
25 Dec – Christmas Day
26 Dec – Boxing Day

Jan–Feb
New Year's Day
1 Jan; Nieuwmarkt and Dam Square
The New Year is ushered in with the consumption of currant-filled doughnuts (*oliebollen* or oil balls) and the launching of fireworks to chase away the evil spirits of the old year.
Commemoration of the 'February Strike'
25 Feb; JD Meijerplein; tel: 020 622 4096; www.februaristaking.nl
Ceremony and speeches in remembrance of the general strike led by the dockers in 1941 against the Nazis' treatment of the Jews.

Mar–Apr
Stille Omgang (Silent Procession)
Sunday closest to 15 Mar; www.stille-omgang.nl
Candlelit procession that begins and ends at Spui.
National Museum Weekend
Mid-Apr; www.museumweekend.nl
State-funded museums offer free or discounted entrance as well as special events.
Koninginnedag (Queen's Day)
30 Apr; city-wide, though with particular focus on the Dam, Vondelpark, the Jordaan and Leidseplein
More than 500,000 people celebrate the birthday of the former queen (Juliana) with street markets, street parties, fireworks and live music throughout the entire city. The initial idea was to create a day on which children could sell their handicrafts, but since the decree allowing anyone to sell anything (within the bounds of legality), the city has become a enormous jumble sale.

May–June
World Press Photo
May–June; Oude Kerk, Oudekerksplein; tel: 020 676 6096; www.worldpressphoto.nl; charge
The world's largest photojournalism competition.
Remembrance Day
4 May; National Monument, Dam
In the presence of the Queen, the ceremony (7.30pm) remembers those who died in World War II.
Liberation Day (Bevrijdingsdag)
5 May; Vondelpark
Celebrations, with live music and speeches, centred primarily around the Vondelpark. The gay commemorations are focused on Museumplein, Leidseplein and Westermarkt.
National Windmill Day
Second Sat in May; tel: 0900 400 4040; www.amsterdamtourist.nl
The sails turn on all 600 statesubsidised windmills as they open their doors to the public.
Open Ateliers: Kunstroute de Westelijke Eilanden
Mid-May; tel: 020 330 4842;

Left: parading dressed as presents at Sinterklass.

www.jordaanfestival.nl
The Jordaan district fills up with brass bands, accordion groups and *smartlap* (tear-jerker music) choirs, and more.

Bock Beer Festival
Late Oct; Beurs van Berlage, Damrak; tel: 020 530 4141; www.beursvanberlage.nl; charge
Three-day beer-tasting event.

Nov–Dec

High Times Cannabis Cup
Mid-Nov; Melkweg, Lijnbaansgracht; www.cannabiscup.com; charge
Five days of events celebrating cannabis culture.

St Nicolaas Parade
Sat in mid-Nov
St Nicolaas arrives by steamer at Centraal Station, together with his Moorish helpers (the Zwarte Pieten), who distribute *pepernoten* (spice biscuits) to the city's children as they proceed up Prins Hendrik-kade to the City Centre.

Sinterklaas
5 Dec
Shops close early so that families can celebrate, exchanging presents and poems in honour of Saint Nicolaas's birthday on 6 December, which is as important to the Dutch as Christmas.

Above: Koninginnedag is always a big celebration.

www.oawe.nl; free
On the tranquil islands around Prinseneiland, resident artists open their studios to visitors over the course of the weekend.

National Cycling Day
Late May; tel: 0900 400 4040; www.amsterdamtourist.nl
Around 200,000 cyclists pedal round 200 designated cycle routes.

Holland Festival
Events at the Stadsschouwburg, Leidseplein and other nearby venues; tel: 020 530 7110; www.holndfstvl.nl; charge
National festival featuring major theatrical, operatic, dance and musical events, many for an English-speaking audience.

July–Aug

Afternoon Concerts and Theatre (Openluchttheather)
July–Aug; Vondelpark; www.vondelpark.nl
Free concerts and theatre are held on summer afternoons and evenings at the open-air pavilion in the Vondelpark. Classical music is also performed on a barge in front of the Pulitzer Hotel.

Gay Pride
First Sat in Aug; www.amsterdampride.nl
Culminates in the afternoon boat parade on Prinsengracht.
SEE ALSO GAY AND LESBIAN, P.61

Uitmarkt
Last weekend of Aug; Museumplein; www.uitmarkt.nl; free
Three-day fair heralding Holland's new cultural season of theatre, music and dance.

Sept–Oct

Jordaan Festival
Third weekend of Sept;

The freezing over of the city's canals is always a major event. The most recent severe freezes occurred in 1985, 1986 and 1997. During a frozen spell, the main event is the Elfstedentocht, a (televised) skating race between 11 towns in the province of Friesland. If you wish to take to the ice yourself, you can do so on the Amsterdamse Bos or in Vondelpark.

Film

Although the international profile of the Netherlands as a centre of filmmaking is not high, the Dutch are, all the same, very keen on cinema. Amsterdam has a wide variety of cinemas and film festivals to cater to every taste, and fortunately for the visitor, foreign films – except some films for children – are almost always screened in their original language (with Dutch subtitles). Weekly programmes change on Thursdays, and you can find out what's showing across the city from either the film agenda listings distributed in cinemas or from www.filmladder.nl.

The Dutch Film Scene

Many people associate Dutch cinema with its distinguished tradition of socially conscious documentary filmmaking. Two of Holland's most famous directors, Joris Ivens and Bert Haanstra, were masters of the genre, although also later branched out into fictional cinema. More recently, other types of film have also received popular, and sometimes critical, acclaim. Look out, in particular, for the action thrillers of Paul Verhoeven, including *Black Book*, which holds the record for the highest-grossing Dutch film to date, the comedies of Martin Koolhoven, the crime capers of Pieter Kuijpers and the quirky reflections of modern Dutch life by Eddy Terstall.

In 2004, while cycling to work, film director **Theo van Gogh** (1957–2004) was shot eight times by a Muslim extremist. The targeting of the outspoken Van Gogh (the great-great-grandson of artist Vincent van Gogh's brother) was related to a short film he had made called *Submission*, which highlighted the violence against women in some Islamic societies. A memorial to the filmmaker can now be found in the city's Oosterpark *(see Parks and Gardens, p.104).*

Film Festivals

Unheard Film Festival
End of Mar; main venue: Kriterion Cinema – see below; www.unheardfilm.nl
Five-day festival devoted to cinema sound design. Dutch indie bands and DJs provide new soundtracks for old films.

Amsterdam Fantastic Film Festival
Apr; Pathé Tuschinski Arthouse – see right; tel: 020 679 4875; www.afff.nl
Fantasy, horror, anime, science fiction and cult films.

Cinedans
Early July; various venues; tel: 06 4213 3812; www.cinedans.nl
Outdoor screenings of films related to dance.

Pluk de Nacht
Aug; various venues; tel: 020 639 2170; www.plukdenacht.nl
Open-air screenings around the city.

Africa in the Picture Festival
Sept; various venues; tel: 020 622 7151; www.africainthepicture.nl
Festival of African film.

Cinekid
Oct; Westergasfabriek, Haarlemmerweg 8–10; tel: 020 6205 230; www.cinekid.nl; Tram: 10; Bus: 18, 22; map p.130 A2
Large festival devoted to films for children – though adults often find it equally enthralling.

International Documentary Filmfestival Amsterdam (IDFA)
Last week of Nov; Pathé Tuschinski and Pathé de Munt – see below; tel: 020 627 3329; www.idfa.nl
The world's largest documentary film festival. See also Shadow Festival (www.shadowfestival.nl), which shows more experimental films.

Arthouse Cinemas (Filmhuizen)

Cinecenter
Lijnbaansgracht 236; tel: 020 623 6615; www.cinecenter.nl; Tram: 1, 5, 7, 10; map p.133 D2
Four-screen arts cinema. Intermissions in films allow you to refill drinks at the bar.

Left: nearly showtime at the Pathé Theater Tuschinski.

To avoid disappointment, book ahead for screenings of popular films at weekends. Tickets for the main cinemas can be purchased online at **www.belbios.nl**, otherwise phone ahead. Be aware that most cinemas do not accept credit cards and some require you to pick up tickets half an hour before the film – otherwise they may be sold on.

Tram: 1, 6; map p.132 C3
Former film academy turned by squatters into a cultural centre with a cinema, radio station and vegan restaurant.

Rialto
Ceintuurbaan 338; tel: 020 676 8700; www.rialtofilm.nl; Tram: 3, 12, 25; map p.133 E4
Stylish neighbourhood cinema with a smart bar and good disabled access.

Multiplexes

Pathé ArenA
ArenA Boulevard 600, Bijlmermeer; tel: 0900 1458; www.pathe.nl; Metro: Bijlmer
Fourteen-screens (including an IMAX) located near the Ajax stadium.

Pathé de Munt
Vijzelstraat 15, Southern Canal Belt; tel: 0900 1458; www.pathe.nl; Tram: 4, 9, 14, 24, 25; map p.136 B4
Seven-screen multiplex in the city centre.

Pathé Theater Tuschinski
Reguliersbreestraat 26–34, Eastern Canal Belt; tel: 0900 1458; www.pathe.nl; Tram: 9, 14, 16, 24; map p.136 B4
Built in 1921, this extravagantly designed cinema sometimes seems more interesting than the blockbuster films. The Pathé Tuschinski Arthouse next door is the reverse: arthouse films, plain décor.

Filmhuis Cavia
Van Hallstraat 51–52; tel: 020 681 1419; www.filmhuiscavia.nl; Tram: 3, 10
Single-screen cinema in a converted school. Specialises in cult, alternative and obscure films.

Het Ketelhuis
Haarlemmerweg 8–10; tel: 020 684 0090; www.ketelhuis.nl; Tram: 10; Bus: 21; map p.130 A2
Boasts an industrial-scale bar.

Kriterion
Roetersstraat 170; tel: 020 623 1708; www.kriterion.nl; Tram: 7, 10; Metro: Weesperplein; map p.134 C3
Founded in 1945 by resistance-fighter undergraduates , the cinema is still run today by students. Films are often followed by debates/discussions. Lively bar.

The Movies
Haarlemmerdijk 161; tel: 020 638 6016; www.themovies.nl; Tram: 3; map p.130 B2
Holland's oldest cinema, established in 1912. The adjoining restaurant offers set dinners with the price of a ticket included.

Nederlands Filmmuseum (NFM)
Vondelpark 3; tel: 020 589 1400; www.filmmuseum.nl; Tram: 1, 2, 10, 12; map p.133 D3
Three-screen cinema attached to the museum. Holds major seasons of classic cinema as well as the less commercial of the contemporary scene. In summer, films are shown outdoors, on the terrace of the Café Vertigo.

OT301
Overtoom 301; tel: 020 779 4913; www.squat.net/overtoom301;

Below: Paul Verhoeven's successful *Black Book*.

53

Food and Drink

It has to be said that Dutch cuisine has never set the world alight, but that doesn't mean that there aren't some great local dishes, food and drink to enjoy while you're in Amsterdam. Cooking tends towards the hearty northern European rather than the more subtle and healthier southern European style, with plenty of stews and soups, and pancakes also popular. There are fewer gourmet restaurants than you might expect in a city this size (not many Michelin stars, for instance), but there's still enough choice whatever your budget, some great street markets, and the spicy dash of Indonesian food too.

Dutch Dishes

You should try to sample a few Dutch specialities while you're in Amsterdam, as food here is generally not too expensive apart from the really smart places. Look out for *stamppot*, which is sausage served with mashed potato and vegetables, or *Hutspot*, a hotpot, a stew usually made with beef and vegetables. A popular warming starter is *erwtensoep* or *snert*, which is a real speciality here: a very thick pea soup that has ham, bacon or sometimes sausage cooked in it. Sausages are popular, as you see, and another dish is *boerenkool met worst*, kale with sausage.

Cheese

The Dutch are known around the world for two fairly bland cheeses, **Gouda** and **Edam** (pronounced 'Ay-dam' not 'Ee-dam'). They're both real places and both easily visited from Amsterdam, and visitors go in their droves to see their cheese markets. The Dutch make hundreds of other cheeses too, like their neighbours the Belgians,

and hardly anyone outside of the Netherlands has heard of any of them. You should try to put that right when you're there, by sampling some of the other varieties in Amsterdam's fine cheese shops *(see p.57)*, or at the street markets where you will invariably find several cheese stalls.

If you like Gouda then try a type called **Leidse**, which has been flavoured with cumin seeds; cumin or cloves are often used to flavour another popular Dutch cheese, **Nagelkaas**. Look for a **Maasdam** too, which is a very rich and smooth cheese a little like **Emmental**.

Left: Edam, one of the best-known Dutch cheeses.

Street Food

By far the most popular street snack in Amsterdam is a helping of **fries** sprinkled with salt and dipped in mayonnaise. This is known as Flemish-style, or *vlaamse*. There are plenty of other dipping options available too, like a rather sweet tomato sauce, curry sauces or the ever-popular satay peanut sauce. Also popular are slices of **raw herring** and other seafood like **smoked eel**, **mussels**, or other fish deep-fried, available from stalls on street corners and bridges around the city.

The Dutch love **pancakes**, and you'll find some stalls making these fresh and offering the usual array of fillings, from sweet to savoury. Cooked fresh and light they are delicious. As a change from Big Macs and KFCs, try **Maoz Falafel**, a Dutch

Right: street food, such as french fries and herring, is very popular.

Left: De Kaaskamer, one of the best cheese shops in the city.

Amsterdam doesn't have an outstanding food market, as many cities do, but most of its street markets have good food stalls selling local as well as international produce. They're the places to go to if you want to buy some Dutch cheese to take home. The **Albert Cuyp-markt** in De Pijp offers the most varied options for dedicated foodies. *See Markets, p.77.*

fast-food chain, or the **FEBO** chain, which is like a cross between a fast-food restaurant and a vending machine. The food's cooked fresh and then loaded into the machines where you choose and put your coins in the slot.

The Indonesian Influence

We tend to think of so-called ethnic foods as being fairly new to the West, but one of the most popular dishes in Amsterdam's Indonesian restaurants, the *rijsttafel*, arrived here in the 17th century with traders from the Dutch East India Company.

There are now numerous Indonesian restaurants all over Amsterdam, their dishes providing a spicy contrast to Dutch food. The *rijsttafel* is a range of small dishes, allowing the chef to show off the menu, and normally they can only be ordered for two people. Some restaurants do offer a *rijsttafel* for one person, and they usually range from about 15–25 dishes. Although they are modest helpings, even a small one is a substantial meal, so take care not to over-order.

Some of the other tasty and popular dishes on the Indonesian menu are satay, the pork kebabs served with or in a spicy peanut sauce, and *gado-gado*, which are cooked, mixed vegetables also served in a peanut sauce.

Dutch Drinking Habits

The Dutch like their beer, and though they're not as famous as their neighbours the Belgians for their brews, you should take the opportunity to sample some of their drinks in Amsterdam. Belgian beers are also widely available, and although Dutch lagers like the famous **Heineken** brand are familiar all over the world, there are plenty of other kinds to try that you won't get elsewhere.

Apart from the top restaurants, most places have fairly

limited wine lists, compared to other countries in Western Europe, but despite the fact that wine is imported it isn't that expensive. The Dutch version of gin, *jenever (see Bars and Cafés, p.33)*, is popular with Amsterdammers, and can be used to start or end a meal, or both, and you should knock it back in one go, not sip it.

The other internationally famous Dutch drink is *advocaat* (eggnog). Made mainly from eggs, sugar and brandy, this thick liqueur is too rich for many people's tastes, especially as it's popularly served with cream on top, and maybe cocoa powder too. It owes its unusual name to the fact that it was originally made not from lawyers, as the old joke goes, but from avocados by Dutch settlers in Surinam. When they returned to the Netherlands they wanted to recreate the taste and texture, and the

closest they could come was by using thickened egg yolks. The new version caught on.

BREWERY TOUR
Heineken Experience
Stadhouderskade 78; tel: 020 523 9666; www.heineken experience.com; daily 11am–7pm; admission charge; Tram: 6, 7, 10; map p.133 E3

The former Heineken brewery in Amsterdam hasn't been a working brewery since 1988, but was instead turned into a tourist attraction. It was recently renovated to include a much more interactive experience than the former brewery tour – though you still get two drinks at the end of it, included in the ticket price. You also get the chance to try brewing your own beer and get a personalised bottle, to learn what it feels like to be a bottle and to star in a music video. There is still the more traditional side

The substantial Surinamese population has brought with it the flavours of the Carribean, such as spicy peanut soup, curries and *rotis*, but another South American culinary contribution you may notice is the prodigious number of steakhouses.

too, like seeing the old brewery works and the brewery's famous shire horses.

Tea and Coffee
You can get tea and coffee anywhere, and have your choice at breakfast, but unless you ask you'll normally get the drink black. Tea will be served without milk but with a slice of lemon, and usually quite weak, so if you want milk with it, ask for a separate carton of milk when you're ordering. Because coffee is also normally served black, fresh milk isn't as widely available as you might expect, and you may have to settle for the long-life variety in cartons, or evaporated milk.

Food and Drink Shops
Albert Heijn
Nieuwezijds Voorburgwal 226; tel: 020 421 8344; www.ah.nl; Mon–Sat 11am–7pm; Tram: 1, 2, 4; map p.136 A2

Albert Heijn is a large Dutch supermarket chain, with over 40 shops in Amsterdam alone. This one near the Dam square is one of the largest, and especially good for food, though the stores do tend to be quite pricey.
Le Cellier
Spuistraat 116; tel: 020 638 6573; www.lecellier.nl; Mon 11am–6pm, Tue–Fri 9.30am–6pm, Sat 9.30am–

Left: organic goodies at Delicious Food.

Left: chocolate heaven at Puccini Bonboni.

5.30pm; Tram: 1, 2, 4; map p.136 A1

Le Cellier has one of the best selections of Dutch *jenever* drinks in the city, but even if you haven't developed a taste for this local liquor, Le Cellier also has a vast array of other spirits and liqueurs from all over the world, including absinthe, and a good range of wines and beers as well.

Delicious Food

Westerstraat 24; tel: 020 320 3070; Mon, Wed–Fri 10am–7pm, Sat 9am–6pm, Sun 11am–3pm; Tram: 3; map p.130 B3

If you want to snack or picnic healthily then this organic indoor market/store is one of the best. It's in the Jordaan, not far from the City Centre, and sells fresh bread, nuts, fruit, bulk items like pasta and rices, and plenty of quick treats you can enjoy alongside one of the nearby canals.

Geels and Co

Warmoesstraat 67; tel: 020 624 0683; www.geels.nl; Mon–Sat 9.30am–6pm; Tram: 4, 9, 14; map p.136 C1

Geels is the kind of shop that is dying out in many city centres, but here in Amsterdam it flourishes right in the middle of the city and has done since 1880. It specialises in teas and coffees, with a huge choice of beans and leaves, and tea- and coffee-making items too.

On Saturdays from 2–4.30pm its little museum of brewing equipment (of the non-alcoholic variety) is open above the shop.

De Kaaskamer

Runstraat 7; tel: 020 623 3483; Mon noon–6pm, Tue–Fri 9am–6pm, Sat 9am–5pm, Sun noon–5pm; Tram: 1, 2, 5; map p.133 D1

This family-run cheese store is very popular with Amsterdammers and always busy. It's here you can find not only the distinctive Edam and Gouda cheeses that you might want to take hone, but also hundreds of other cheeses from the Netherlands and all over the world. You can also buy cold meats, pâtés, olives and everything you need for a picnic lunch.

Puccini Bomboni

Staalstraat 17; tel: 020 626 5474; www.puccinibomboni.com; Sun–Mon noon–6pm, Tue–Sat 9am–6pm; Metro: Waterlooplein; map p.136 C4

Sample anything from Amsterdam's most famous chocolate-maker and you'll know why chocoholics think it's worth coming to the city just to buy here. The chocs are handmade on the premises, with no artificial ingredients used, and there's a mouth-watering variety of flavours available including

such unusual options as rhubarb, prune, pepper, gin and lemon grass. There's another branch of the store at **Singel 184** (tel: 020 427 8341), with the same opening hours apart from closing an hour earlier on Sunday.

Waterwinkel

Roelof Hartstraat 10; tel: 020 675 5932; www.springwater.nl; Mon–Fri 10am–6pm, Sat 10am–5pm; Tram: 3, 24; map p.133 D4

If you get thirsty visiting the museums on the Museumplein then just south of here is the place to quench your thirst... and your curiosity. Waterwinkel sells water and only water, and it's guaranteed you never knew water came in so many different varieties and bottles.

Wegewijs

Rozengracht 32; tel: 020 624 4093; www.wegewijs.nl; Mon–Fri 8.30am–6pm, Sat 9am–5pm; Tram: 13, 14, 17; map p.130 A4

This is another delightful place to discover more about the impressive variety of Dutch cheese, and if you're not familiar with Dutch styles you can try before you buy. It's also a very good general delicatessen with pâtés, salads, fruit and fresh bread, so you can put together the ideal lunch if you fancy a picnic.

Right: at Albert Heijn.

Gay and Lesbian

Amsterdam is one of the most gay-friendly cities in the world, thanks to its longstanding relaxed and tolerant attitudes. There are gay bars galore, many hotels that cater specifically to gay visitors, clubs, saunas, parties – basically anything you're interested in can probably be found in Amsterdam. As well as events like Gay Pride, the gay community joins in many of the city's big events with gusto, such as the Queen's birthday on 30 April. Gay culture here is a part of the mainstream culture, and it isn't surprising that Amsterdam is where the world's first same-sex marriage was celebrated, in 2002.

Accommodation

Amsterdam is generally a pretty gay-friendly place, so it's hard to single out particular hotels, though the ones below have actively encouraged gay and lesbian guests.

Amistad
Kerkstraat 42; tel: 020 624 8074; www.amstad.nl; €–€€; Tram: 1, 2, 5; map p.133 E1
Not far from the bar and club scene around the Leidseplein, the Amistad's American owners Jerry and Steve know all the gay-friendly drinking places, clubs, saunas, cafés and places for gay parties. It's an amazing bargain, as the rooms are stylish and they

Price ranges, which are given as a guide only, are for a standard double room with bathroom in peak season, including service and tax but excluding breakfast. Breakfast usually costs from around €7–15 depending on the rating of the hotel.

€€€€	over €300
€€€	€150–300
€€	€100–150
€	under €100

all have a PC with free high-speed internet.

Black Tulip
Geldersekade 16; tel: 020 427 0933; www.blacktulip.nl; €€; Metro: Centraal Station; map p.137 C1
A short walk from Centraal Station on the way to the Red Light District, the Black Tulip describes itself as Europe's most luxurious art and leather hotel – and they're not just talking about the sofas. Most hotel rooms these days have TVs and now DVDs, but at the Black Tulip there are S&M facilities too.

Golden Bear
Kerkstraat 37; tel: 020 624 8074; www.goldenbear.nl; €–€€; Tram: 1, 2, 5; map p.133 E2
Just down the road from the Amistad, the Golden Bear is also close to lots of the city's gay bars and other hangouts. It was Amsterdam's first gay hotel when it opened way back in 1948, in two 18th-century buildings, and it does have the luxury of spacious rooms if you can negotiate the steep and narrow stairs.

ITC Hotel
Prinsengracht 1051; tel: 020 623 0230; www.itc-hotel.com; €; Tram: 4; map p.134 A3
A dull name for a lovely hotel in an attractive and historic building on the Prinsengracht canal. Many of the rooms overlook the canal; there's a bar, a light and airy breakfast room, free internet, a breakfast buffet until noon, and all for a bargain price.

Advice and Information

Gay and Lesbian Switchboard
tel: 020 623 6565; www.switchboard.nl
For information on any aspect of gay life in Amsterdam, or for help if you need it.

COC
Rozenstraat 8, 1016 NX Amsterdam; tel: 020 623 4596; www.coc.nl
Information is available from the national organisation **COC** (Cultuur en Ontspannings-Centrum, or Centre for Culture and Leisure) which

Right: choices for sleeping and S&M at the Black Tulip 'art and leather' hotel.

Left: crowds at the gay bar ARC spill out onto the street.

lesbian life in the city. It's very close to the Anne Frank Huis *(see Museums and Galleries, p.80)* too, so easy to find. And if you want a novelty gay souvenir, you'll find plenty of fun choices here.

Bars and Cafés

ARC
Reguliersdwarsstraat 44; tel: 020 689 7070; www.bararc.com; Sun–Thur 4pm–1am, Fri–Sat 4pm–3am; free; Tram: 1, 2, 4; map p.136 A4
This upmarket bar may be pricey, but it's always packed at the weekend, predominantly with good-looking gay and bi- guys enjoying the good food and drinks, and the music.

Lellebel
Utrechtsestraat 4; tel: 020 427 5139; www.lellebel.nl; Mon–Thur 9pm–3am, Fri–Sat 8pm–4am, Sun 3pm–3am; admission charge; Tram: 4, 9, 14; map p.134 A2
Since Lellebel, which is more of a small bar, opened in 1997 it has become incredibly popular for its live drag shows, although the

was founded in 1946, and claims to be the oldest organisation in the world that caters to the lesbian, gay, bisexual and transgender communities.

Pink Point
Westermarkt; tel: 020 428 1070; www.pinkpoint.org; daily 10am–6pm; Tram: 13, 14, 17; map p.130 B4
This gay and lesbian information centre is in a booth on the corner of Raadhuisstraat and Keizersgracht, near the **Homomonument** *(see p.61)* at the Westmarkt. It started life as a converted ice-cream cart during Amsterdam's 1998 Gay Games, and after spells being housed in a shipping container and a flower stall, it is now one of the city's main information kiosks for both visitors and locals. This is the place to pick up any of the newspapers, magazines and maps *(see p.61)*, and flyers and other information about anything to do with gay and

Left above: a drag show at Café Lellebel *(see p.59)* and **Left below:** the Cockring.

Sappho

Vijzelstraat 103; tel: 020 423 1509; www.sappho.nl; Sun–Thur 3pm–1am, Fri–Sat 3pm–3am; free; Tram: 16, 24, 25; map p.133 E2

Another relaxed café-bar that's mainly for lesbians but has a relaxed attitude, and there are plenty of gay men, bisexual and straight people too. The entertainment is just as wide-ranging too, with comedy nights, open-mike nights for singer/songwriters, DJs, bands, movies and plays – anything could be happening, so check the website or the listings magazines for the current programme.

Sugar

Hazenstraat 19; tel: 020 486 5433; Mon, Wed–Fri 4pm–1am, Sat–Sun 4pm–3am; admission charge; Tram: 7, 10, 17; map p.133 D1

Relaxed and friendly, predominantly (but not exclusively) lesbian bar in the Jordaan, that starts to pick up more of a club atmosphere as the night progresses.

Clubs

Cockring

Warmoesstraat 96; tel: 020 623 9604; www.clubcockring.com; daily 11pm–late; admission charge on Sat and for special events; Tram: 4, 9, 16; map p.136 B1

One of the most famous gay clubs in the city, and one of the first to be open seven days a week. It's not the kind of place the unwary visitor would wander into by mistake. This is just as well, as

You don't have to wear drag – it's a very relaxed place – but you'll be in a minority if you don't.

Pub Soho

Reguliersdwarsstraat 36; tel: 020 638 5700; www.pub soho.eu; Mon–Thur, Sun 6pm–2am, Fri–Sat 6pm–4am; free; Tram: 1, 2, 4; map p.136 A4

Going for the British pub look, the Soho on the gay-friendly Reguliersdwarsstraat is open to everyone but attracts mainly a male crowd. It's a great place for relaxing with some friends and a few beers, though there are also DJs and live bands for dancing too, mainly at the weekends.

Saarein II

Elandsstraat 19; tel: 020 623 4901; www.saarein.nl; Tue–Thur, Sun 5pm–1am, Fri 5pm–2am, Sat noon–4pm, 5pm–2am; free; Tram: 7, 10, 17; map p.133 D1

This Jordaan bar was the first women-only bar in the city and was renowned as a radical feminist/lesbian meeting place. Today it's open to all and is more of a place to relax and have a beer, meet people and play a few bar games. There's food available too, and it recently started opening for Saturday lunch.

cross-dressing customers provide their own entertainment when there's nothing else happening. There are regular karaoke nights, salsa nights, occasional themes like Indonesian evenings, and drag open-mike nights.

Although for the most part Amsterdam is incredibly gay-friendly, every city in the world experiences incidences of gay folk being beaten up, sometimes killed, in violent acts. Sometimes these are random, sometimes not, but although there are far fewer of these incidents than in many places, gay men in particular should still be on their guard and monitor their behaviour, and take the usual safety precautions if in unknown neighbourhoods.

Right: girls' fun at Sappho.

the action can get very steamy, especially during the occasional Sunday sex parties, which are not for the faint-hearted.

Exit
Reguliersdwarsstraat 42; tel: 020 638 5700; www.clubexit.eu; Thur, Sun 11pm–4am, Fri, Sat 11pm–5am; admission charge (Fri–Sat only); Tram: 1, 2, 4; map p.136 A4

Huge music club on several levels and with different styles on each, including R&B and disco pop. Live entertainment some nights too, with bands, singers and strippers.

Events

Amsterdam Gay Pride
www.amsterdamgaypride.nl
Takes place on the first weekend each August, and is one of the biggest and most fun gay pride events in Europe. The Canal Parade is one of the event's biggest attractions, which everybody – gay or straight – can enjoy.

Leather Pride
www.leatherpride.nl
Held in October/November, this is a more outrageous and hardcore event.

Transgender Film Festival
www.transgenderfilmfestival.com
Every other May in odd-numbered years, this takes place over several days.

Media

IN PRINT
Gay Map to Amsterdam
www.gayamsterdam.com
Gay News Amsterdam
www.gaynews.nl
Gay & Night
www.gay-night.nl
Find these publications on newsstands or in some of the gay bars and clubs listed here. *Amsterdam Weekly* (www.amsterdamweekly.nl) has a listings section for gay and lesbian events in the city each week.

ON THE AIR
Dutch radio and TV caters specifically for its gay audience through **MVS** (www.mvs.nl), a broadcasting company that puts out programmes on MVS Radio (106.8 FM) and MVS TV (on cable).

ONLINE
Gay.nl (www.gay.nl) is a multilingual online magazine that is part of a wider European network, and incredibly informative about the Amsterdam gay scene.

Monument

Homomonument
Westermarkt; Tram: 13, 14, 17; map p.130 B4
In the concentration camps of the Nazis during World War II, gay men were forced to wear a pink triangle on their uniforms to identify themselves. In 1987 in Amsterdam, three large pink triangles made of granite and forming a larger triangle were built into the ground near the Westerkerk church on the Keizersgracht canal to commemorate all gay men and women who have been persecuted anywhere because of who they are. The three triangles, designed by Dutch artist Karin Daan to symbolise the past, the present and the future, now fulfil that symbolism by commemorating past victims, acting as a rallying point during events like Gay Pride, and looking forward to a more tolerant future. It is typical of Amsterdam that when it was unveiled, this was the first sculpture of its kind in the world.

History

C.1200
The first communities of herring fishermen settle on the banks of the Amstel. The first dam, or sluice, is built to hold back the tidal waters of the Zuiderzee.

1300
The Bishop of Utrecht grants Amsterdam official city status.

1519
As a result of war, treaties and marriage alliances, Amsterdam is part of the Spanish Empire and nominally Catholic, but tolerant of Protestants (persecuted throughout Europe).

1535
Anabaptists invade the town hall to proclaim the Second Coming. The occupiers are arrested and executed. Catholicism is reimposed.

1566
The Iconoclastic Fury (*Beeldenstorm*). Calvinists protesting at the lack of religious freedom storm many of Amsterdam's churches.

1567
Philip II of Spain sends the Duke of Alva to restore Catholic control of Amsterdam. Many Protestants are executed or flee to England.

1572
The Dutch Revolt against Spanish rule begins in earnest, led by William of Orange.

1578
Amsterdam capitulates to Prince William. Protestant exiles return to the city. Calvinists take over the churches and the reins of government in the peaceful Alteration (*Alteratie*) revolution.

1579
The seven northern provinces of the Netherlands sign the Treaty of Utrecht providing for mutual assistance in the event of attack. Protestant refugees from Antwerp, Amsterdam's trade rival, seek asylum in the city and help to lay the foundations for the Golden Age.

1602
The United Dutch East India Company is established to coordinate trade with the lands east of the Cape of Good Hope, financed by a public share flotation.

1609
The Bank of Amsterdam is formed, placing the city at the forefront of European finance. Hendrik Staets draws up the plan for the Grachten-gordel, the three concentric canals ringing the city.

1626
Peter Minuit 'buys' the island of Manhattan and founds the colony of Nieuw Amsterdam (taken by the English and renamed New York in 1664).

1648
The Treaty of Münster recognises the northern provinces as an independent republic.

1688
William III of Holland is crowned as King of England, having married the Stuart Queen Mary II. William's wars against the French strain the Dutch economy and the republic's trade begins to decline.

1702
William III dies without an heir. Amsterdam and the northern provinces suffer further inroads into their trade when the Austrian Emperor Charles VI sets up a rival East India Company in Ostend.

1744
France invades the southern provinces.

1747
William IV is elected hereditary head of state of the seven northern provinces, now unified under one leader and called the United Provinces.

1751–88
The United Provinces are torn between conservative supporters of the House of Orange and liberal reformers, called Patriots.

1795

France invades Amsterdam and, in alliance with the Patriots, forms a National Assembly. The United Provinces are named the Batavian Republic.

1806

Napoleon reverses the constitutional reforms and establishes his brother, Louis, as King of Holland, with Amsterdam as its capital.

1813

After the defeat of Napoleon, William VI is welcomed back to Amsterdam from exile.

1814

William VI is crowned King William I of the Netherlands.

1914–20

The Netherlands remains neutral during World War I, but food shortages lead to strikes, riots and support for the Dutch Communist Party.

1928

Amsterdam hosts the Olympic Games.

1940

Germany ignores the neutrality of the Netherlands and invades on 10 May.

1941

Over 400 Jews are rounded up in Amsterdam on 22 and 23 February. Dockworkers lead a two-day strike in protest at anti-Jewish measures.

1942

Anne Frank and family go into hiding.

1945

After a bitter winter Amsterdam is liberated.

1965

The Provos (provocateurs), a anarchist protest movement dedicated to shaking Dutch complacency, win representation on the city council.

1994

400th anniversary of the first tulip to be grown in Holland.

1998

The first Gay Games attract thousands of visitors.

2002

Crown Prince Willem Alexander weds Argentinian Máxima Zorreguieta at the city's Nieuwe Kerk, and the world's first same-sex marriage with an identical legal status to heterosexual marriage takes place in Amsterdam.

2004

After making a film critical of Islam, director Theo van Gogh is murdered in Amsterdam. Anti-Muslim violence breaks out across the country.

2005

The Netherlands votes against the EU constitution.

2006

Prime Minister Balkenende's centre-right coalition collapses in a row over immigration. General election in November.

2007

After the general election, Jan Peter Balkenende is sworn in as head of a three-party coalition in February.

2008

New Conservatory of Amsterdam opens. Four halls offer free music concerts almost daily.

Hotels

The pleasure of visiting Amsterdam begins with choosing a hotel. It's a small city, but it offers a wide choice of characterful and colourful places to stay, from canal barges to homely guesthouses to grand hotels to the latest in chic and boutique-style properties. In some cities like London and Paris you have to stay out of the centre to bag a bargain, but this is not the case in Amsterdam. There are hotels for all budgets right in the middle of the city, and the choice is not so much where to stay as what to stay in – a quirky B&B, a bike-friendly place, a historic building or plain old plush luxury.

City Centre

Grand Hotel Krasnapolsky

Dam 9; tel: 020 554 9111; www.nh-hotels.com; €€€€; Tram: 4, 9, 14; map p.136 B2

Facing the Royal Palace on Dam Square, the Krasnapolsky is also a pretty good Amsterdam address. If you want the prestige without the price, there are often good deals on some of the rooms, and you can indulge yourself in the fitness centre, Jacuzzi, courtyard, bars, lounges or the Belle Epoque Reflet restaurant.

Hotel Brouwer

Singel 83; tel: 020 624 6358; www.hotelbrouwer.nl; €;

Tram: 1, 2, 5; map p.136 A1

You don't have to pay a fortune to get a room with a canal view in Amsterdam – in that respect it is not the Venice of the north. The Brouwer has been run by the same family since 1917, and its upper rooms under the eaves have fantastic views. At this bargain price there are no frills, but you do get breakfast included and a warm welcome.

Hotel de l'Europe

Nieuwe Doelenstraat 5; tel: 020 531 1777; www.leurope.nl; €€€€; Tram: 4, 9, 14: map p.136 B4

Left: a charming and colourful room at Hotel Misc.

This is about as central as you can get, whether you want the Red Light District, the Rijksmuseum or the Rembrandthuis. There's a pool and fitness centre, two restaurants, and to drink or dine on the terrace overlooking the Amstel is a true Amsterdam indulgence.

Hotel Estheréa

Singel 303–309; tel: 020 624 5146; www.estherea.nl; €€€; Tram: 1, 2, 5; map p.136 A3

Despite having 71 rooms spread over several canal houses, the Estherea seems much more intimate. It's been chosen as one of the top romantic hotels in the city, and the rooms have a warmth and elegance about them, with marble bathrooms and some with four-poster beds.

Hotel Sint Nicolaas

Spuistraat 1a; tel: 020 626 1384; www.hotelnicolaas.nl; €€; Tram: 1, 2 5; map p.130 C3

If you want cheap and central, a couple of minutes from Centraal Station, this very friendly 3-star spot with 27

Left: the Blue Room at the quirky Kamer 01 *(see p.68)*.

Amsterdam is a compact city, and most major attractions can be reached on foot or by tram. It doesn't matter too much which district you stay in, but some areas, like the Red Light District and the Leidseplein area, can be rowdy at night. The Jordaan is more relaxing, and still close enough to the centre of the city.

the compensations are a terrific atmosphere, helpful staff, old-world charm and its central location.

France
Oudezijds Kolk 11; tel: 020 535 3777; www.francehotel.nl; €€€; Metro: Centraal Station; map p.137 C1

No mistaking this place with its French flag outside, while inside are 55 recently renovated rooms, done out mainly in primary colours for a bright, modern feel. They're also kept spotlessly clean, and you can pay extra for a canal view.

Hotel Misc
Kloveniersburgwal 20; tel: 020 330 6241; www.hotelmisc.com; €€€; Metro: Nieuwmarkt; map p.136 C2

This is the hotel you're always hoping to find – central but

inexpensive rooms is it. It's recently been smartened up: there's nothing that could really be done about the small rooms, but other than that it's a real bargain.

Sofitel The Grand Amsterdam
Oudezijds Voorburgwal 197; tel: 020 555 3111; www.thegrand.nl; €€€€; Tram: 4, 9, 14; map p.136 B3

Most cities have a Grand hotel and this is Amsterdam's, formerly the town hall. Now it's seriously swish, with an indoor pool, sauna, spa, rooms with perfect canal views and a gourmet French restaurant.

Nieuwmarkt and the Red Light District

Bellevue Hotel
Martelaarsgracht 10; tel: 020 707 4500; www.embhotels.nl; €€; Metro: Centraal Station; map p.130 C3

Close to Centraal Station and Damrak, the rooms at this simple hotel are small, but modern and cheerfully

decorated in bright colours or plain white. It's got its own bistro and pub on the ground floor, and the area can be noisy at night. Nevertheless, the hotel is very well run and good value.

Doelen
Nieuwe Doelenstraat 24; tel: 020 554 0600; www.nh-hotels.com; €€€; Tram: 4, 9, 16; map p.136 B4

This 17th-century building on the banks of the Amstel has its own jetty, and inside the building there's a Baroque feel to it. Some rooms are inevitably small, in a building of this age, but

Right: a bright room with a view at the Bellevue Hotel.

Left: the bar and a 'Klasbols' room at the Dylan Amsterdam.

Amsterdam, and any hotel to choose from, the Dylan would be it. This 17th-century canal house where Vivaldi once conducted now discreetly hosts visiting VIPs. Its courtyard buffers guests from the bustle, its rooms are all uniquely stylish – and it's worth it.

't Hotel
Leliegracht 18; tel: 020 422 2741; www.thotel.nl; €€; Tram: 13, 17; map p.130 B4

Hard to believe that 't Hotel is only 3-star, as its eight rooms are all superb, several with canal views and the top-floor Amstel sleeping up to eight people with a ladder up to the loft room under the eaves. It's stylish but homely, and the room rate includes breakfast.

Hotel Pulitzer
Prinsengracht 315–331; tel: 020 523 5235; www.starwood hotels.com; €€€€; Tram: 13, 14, 17; map p.133 D1

The Pulitzer has not one but two canals for its guest rooms to overlook, and it's a luxurious warren of a place built from 25 canal houses. The result is a place that oozes charm and character, and despite having 230 rooms it still seems very personal, a place where you feel that every guest genuinely matters.

Hotel van Onna
Bloemgracht 102/104/108; tel: 020 626 5801; www.hotel vanonna.nl; €; Tram: 13, 14, 17; map p.130 A4

The owner, Loek van Onna, was born in one of the three canal houses that make up his hotel, so it has a very homely feel to it. The rooms are fairly spartan, as you might expect at this budget price, though breakfast is

quiet, intimate (six rooms), well run, comfortable and affordable. It's close to but not in the Red Light District, in a 17th-century canal house, with free wifi and breakfast, king-size beds, and the front rooms are larger with canal views.

Western Canal Belt and the Jordaan

Acacia
Lindengracht 251; tel: 020 622 1460; www.hotelacacia.nl; €; Bus: 18; map p.130 A3

The Acacia is everything you want for a real Amsterdam stay – a quirky canalside house in a relaxed Jordaan neighbourhood, friendly owners, strangely shaped rooms, lots of stairs, and the option to stay on their houseboat if you prefer.

Dylan Amsterdam
Keizersgracht 384; tel: 020 530 2010; www.dylanamsterdam.com; €€€€; Tram: 1, 2, 5; map p.133 D1

Given one last night in

Although it is a popular tourist destination, Amsterdam's compact nature means that there are fewer hotel rooms than in most major cities. If you are planning to travel at a busy period, you should book well ahead. That said, most Amsterdam hotels are reasonably priced. If you arrive with no accommodation booked, head for the tourist information office of the VVV, right outside Centraal Station. It operates a hotel-booking service, with a small charge for making the booking. It does get very busy – another reason for booking ahead wherever possible.

Watch out for accommodation touts as you emerge from Centraal Station onto the busy square in front of it, Stationsplein. Linger too long here and you'll be offered almost anything for sale. While some of the people are genuine, others are not, and why take the risk when you can walk into the tourist information office of the VVV, also on Stationsplein, and book something there perfectly safely?

included and if you don't mind the stairs, the higher rooms offer good views.

Southern Canal Belt and Leidseplein

Dikker & Thijs Fenice
Prinsengracht 444; tel: 020 620 1212; www.dtfh.nl; €€; Tram: 1, 2, 5; map p.133 D2
Ask for a room with a canal view, as you don't want to be at the rear of this 18th-century former warehouse. Most rooms are spacious too, the décor a little old-fashioned, and it's worth paying for breakfast at least once to sample the exposed wood and stained glass in the dining room.

Eden Amsterdam American Hotel
Leidsekade 97; tel: 020 556 3000; www.edenamsterdam americanhotel.com; €€; Tram: 1, 2, 5; map p.133 D2
For a long time the American, an Art Deco monument built in 1900, lived on its laurels. Recently, however, there have been great improvements. The public areas have always been good, and now the rooms are being brought up to scratch. Some are small, but most have good views to compensate, and it's

worth paying for a better room if you can.

Hotel Leydsche Hof
Leidsegracht 14; tel: 020 638 2327; www.freewebs.com/leydschehof; €€; Tram: 1, 2, 5; map p.133 E2
A typical relaxed Amsterdam stay is in a place like this, where someone's home has been converted into a small hotel. This 17th-century house on a quieter canal has seven rooms that are homely in the best sense of the word, and the very reasonable room rates also include breakfast.

Hotel Seven One Seven
Prinsengracht 717; tel: 020 427 0717; www.717hotel.nl; €€€€; Tram: 1, 2 5; map p.133 E2
From the outside the 717 looks like a lawyer's office, but inside is the ultimate indulgent guesthouse. From the arty Picasso Suite to the OTT Stravinsky Room with its own piano, here are eight enormous suites where the room rates include breakfast, afternoon tea, drinks from the

mini-bar and your choice of house wines.

Eastern Canal Belt and Rembrandtplein

Banks Mansion
Herengracht 519–525; tel: 020 420 0055; www.banks mansion.nl; €€€; Tram: 16, 24, 25; map p.133 E2
The rates here, in what was once an old bank, include not only breakfast but drinks (even from the mini-bar), snacks that you'll find in the hotel lounge and free internet. The building is impressive, though some rooms are

Right: the Banks Mansion is in an ideal location by a canal.

67

as small as a bank safe, but the location's perfect.

Hotel de Munck

Achtergracht 3; tel: 020 623 6283; www.hoteldemunck.com; €€; Tram: 4, 6, 7; map p.134 B3

It sometimes seems like there's no such thing as a regular Amsterdam hotel, and here the reception is done up in 1960s style, complete with a jukebox. The rooms are more conventional, simple 2-star standard, the plus points being the friendliness of the staff and the complimentary Dutch buffet breakfast.

Hotel Orlando

Prinsengracht 1099; tel: 020 638 6915; www.hotelorlando.nl; €€; Tram: 4; map p.134 A3

With only five rooms spread over three floors, the Orlando offers that rare Amsterdam treat – space. The canalside building is 17th-century but the rooms are stylishly modern, set off by a few traditional touches like antique wardrobes. Choose from a canal, a courtyard or a garden view.

Kamer 01

Derde Weteringdwarsstraat 44; tel: 020 625 6627; www.kamer01.nl; €€€; Tram: 16, 25, 25; map p.133 E3

If you want quality personal service, it doesn't come better than a two-room boutique hotel in a 17th-century building. The Blue Room has a

Price ranges, which are given as a guide only, are for a standard double room with bathroom in peak season, including service and tax but excluding breakfast. Breakfast usually costs from around €7–15 depending on the rating of the hotel.

€€€€	over €300
€€€	€150–300
€€	€100–150
€	under €100

round bed and small private terrace, while the Red Room has a king-size bed, and both rooms (did you guess the colour schemes?) have Apple iMacs, flatscreen TVs and DVD players. Utter indulgence.

Seven Bridges

Reguliersgracht 31; tel: 020 623 1329; http://sevenbridgeshotel.nl; €€; Tram: 4; map p.134 A2

Rates include breakfast in bed or just in your room, as there's no dining room, but what excellent, friendly service you get. There are only eight rooms, all showing the owners' love for antiques, well suited to this 300-year-old canalside house. Archetypal Amsterdam.

The Museum Quarter, Vondelpark and the South

Bilderberg Hotel Jan Luyken

Jan Luijkenstraat 58; tel: 020 573 0730; www.janluyken.nl; €€; Tram: 2, 5; map p.133 D3

The Bilderberg's 19th-century exterior hides a secret – a stylish boutique-style hotel, with its own little spa and rooms that can be small but with soothing dark tones, while the wine bar feels like having your own private club. A top choice.

The College Hotel

Roelof Hartstraat 1; tel: 020 571 1511; www.collegehotel amsterdam.com; €€€; Tram: 3, 12; map p.133 D4

Amsterdammers not only have great ideas, they carry them out really well. How about a truly luxurious hotel, staffed by students from the city's hotel and catering college? That's the College, housed in an 1894 university building, with cool rooms, some decorated on modern minimalist lines and others sumptuously decadent. The restaurant's top-notch too.

Fusion Suites Number 40

Roemer Visscherstraat 40; tel: 020 618 4642; www.fusion suites.com; €€€; Tram: 1, 3, 12; map p.133 D3

One of the best boutique hotels in the city. The rooms are all different – some traditional with antique touches, some light and airy, others fun and colourful – but they're all spacious and the complimentary breakfast fantastic. For an absolutely guaranteed special stay in Amsterdam, this is the place.

Hotel Fita

Jan Luijkenstraat 37; tel: 020 679 0976; www.fita.nl; €€; Tram: 2, 5; map p.133 D3

This is a true family hotel, well run by Hans and Loes de Rapper, who get repeat business by offering free

Right: the fantastic view from a room at the Seven Bridges.

Left: space and elegance at the Fusion Suites.

The rooms at the artsy Vondel have all been differently designed – some are cool and simple, others busy and funky, with lots of artworks around the place. There's a nice garden for sunny-day breakfasts, and it's close to both the Vondelpark and Van Gogh Museum.

Sandton Hotel de Filosoof

Anna Van den Vondelstraat 6; tel: 020 683 3013; www.hotel filosoof.nl; €€; Tram: 1, 3, 12; map p.132 C3

Another quirky but endearing Amsterdam place: a hotel devoted to philosophy. It's in a late 19th-century house by the Vondelpark, and each room is designed in the style of philosophers from Confucius to Wittgenstein. Amazingly, it works, and the standards belie the 3-star rating and the price. Uniquely excellent.

Jodenbuurt, the Plantage and the Oost

Bridge Hotel

Amstel 107–111; 020 623 7068; www.thebridgehotel.nl; €; Tram: 9; map p.134 B3

This is a privately owned three-star hotel, and it's worth paying extra to get a

> Some Amsterdam hotels are notoriously difficult for people with mobility problems. The tall canalside houses don't usually have elevators, but instead they have narrow, twisting staircases that are almost vertical and present challenges to most people. It is essential that travellers with disabilities check before making a reservation. *See also Essentials, p.46.*

room on a higher floor with a view and away from the street. The most spacious rooms are the self-catering apartments, if you're wanting a longer stay in the city.

Hotel Adolesce

Nieuwe Keizersgracht 26; tel: 020 626 3959; www.adolesce.nl; €; Tram: 4, 6, 7; map p.134 B2

This 10-room hotel near the Skinny Bridge (so a bit out of the centre) is one of the city's best bargains. Though it's a budget choice, the owners provide free drinks and snacks all day in the lounge (making it popular with families), and while the rooms are pretty basic they're immaculate.

Hotel Arena

's Gravesandestraat 51; tel: 020 850 2410; www.hotelarena.nl; €; Tram: 7, 10; map p.134 C3

internet, free European and US phone calls, a great breakfast, friendly smiles, and 15 simple but spotless non-smoking rooms. A little gem, near the Van Gogh Museum.

Hotel Vondel

Vondelstraat 28–30; tel: 020 612 0120; www.hotelvondel. com; €€€; Tram: 1, 3, 12; map p.133 D3

Left: modern design as befits the area at the Movenpick.

cious rooms, friendly service and a great antique-style breakfast room.

The Waterfront

Lloyd Hotel

Oostelijke Handelskade 34; tel: 020 561 3636; www.lloyd hotel.com; €€–€€€€; Tram: 10, 26

There is nowhere like the Lloyd, which cannot be categorised. It calls itself a 'Hotel and Cultural Embassy', and rooms range from 1-star to 5-star. It's a huge docklands building where something's always going on – art event, party, business conference or even a '60s-style 'Happening'. It's cheap, it's pricey, it's funky, it's stylish.

Movenpick

Piet Heinkade 11; tel: 020 519 1200; www.movenpick-hotels.com; €€€; Tram: 25, 26; map p.131 E3

Why pick a modern Moven-pick in old Amsterdam? Because it's on the water-front and the views are fantastic, and while from the outside it looks bland, inside the rooms are stylishly simple, with the creature comforts some of the more 'characterful' city hotels lack.

De Pijp

Hotel Okura Amsterdam

Ferdinand Bolstraat 333; tel: 020 678 7111; www.okura.nl; €€€; Tram: 12, 25

This is the gourmet's choice, with its French **Ciel Bleu** restaurant having two Michelin stars, the **Yamazato** with one Michelin star and also the Tep-panyaki restaurant Sazanka, where food is grilled at your table. There's a pool, health club, beauty salon and plush,

There are plenty of cheap hostels and dorms in Amsterdam – it attracts a lot of backpackers – and though there are some dives you stand a better chance of finding somewhere decent here than in many cities. Some appeal to cyclists, some to Christians, and some to backpackers. Some have only dorms, while others offer private rooms too. Try the **Bulldog Hotel** (www.bulldoghotel.com), which is part of the company better-known for its coffee-shops, while the **Flying Pig** (www.flyingpig.nl) has two backpackers' hostels. **Stayokay** (www.stayokay.com) has three in Amsterdam and many more throughout the Netherlands.

This late 19th-century orphanage now comprises a hotel, a restaurant and a nightclub under one roof, and if staying there you'd better like black and white, after a 2008 makeover on the rooms. It's hip and it's a little out of the centre, but you'll have a real Amsterdam experience if you choose to stay here.

Hotel Rembrandt

Plantage Middenlaan 17; tel: 020 627 2714; www.hotel rembrandt.nl; €€; Tram: 9, 14; map p.137 E4

Located in the pleasant Plantage neighbourhood, not far from the Rem-brandthuis, you get more than you pay for at the Rem-brandt – spotless and spa-

modern rooms. Top class.

SEE ALSO RESTAURANTS, P.112

Hotel Savoy
Ferdinand Bolstraat 194;
tel: 020 644 7445;
www.savoyhotel.nl; €€€;
Tram: 3, 12, 16

The 4-star Savoy has had a
makeover like the surrounding Pijp district and joined
the all-inclusive club, where
your room rate gets you free
drinks, snacks and internet,
and your personal host
rather than a mere recep-
tionist. Rooms are artily
modern, small but decked
out in a fun fashion.

Van Ostade Bicycle Hotel
Van Ostadestraat 123; tel: 020
679 3452; www.bicycle
hotel.com; €; Tram: 3, 12, 25;
map p.134 A4

This is pure Amsterdam –
bicycle-friendly (you can hire
bikes here), cosy, inexpensive, solar-powered, full of
character. Breakfast and
internet are both free, the
rooms are basic but very
comfortable, and little wonder that those on a budget
book well in advance.

Beyond Amsterdam

Carlton Square Hotel
Baan 7, Haarlem; tel: 023 531
9091; www.carlton.nl; €€

The Carlton Square is a
4-star hotel whose rooms
are done out in a plush classical style, oozing comfort,
but with modern facilities
like wifi. Dining in their
restaurant De La Paix is
fun, with its open kitchen,
and the hundreds of
whiskies on the Whisky
Bar menu are definitely a
late-night temptation.

Hotel de Kok
Houttuinen 14, Delft;
tel: 015 212 2125;

www.hoteldekok.nl; €
You know a hotel
looks after its guests
when it provides a shed
for people's bikes. The
de Kok is full of little
touches like this, and
though the rooms are
fairly simple, front ones
overlook the canal and
rear ones the hotel's lovely
garden, with its fountain
and colourful flowers.

Right: luxurious bathrooms
and spa facilities at the Hotel
Okura Amsterdam.

Language

Eavesdropping on any Dutch conversation, you could be forgiven for thinking that Dutch people constantly need to clear their throat! This Germanic language regularly uses a guttural consonant similar to the 'ch' in the Scottish word 'loch'. In Dutch terms this is known as the 'soft g', although the 'hard g' sounds almost the same – if you look at Dutch words that begin with a 'g', then you can reasonably assume the word starts with that infamous 'ch'. Any attempt you make at speaking Dutch will be received as a compliment. To this end, here are a some useful Dutch words and phrases.

General

How much is it?
Hoeveel is het?/Hoeveel kost dit?

What is your name?
Wat is uw naam?

My name is...
Mijn naam is...

Do you speak English?
Spreekt u Engels?

I am English/American
Ik ben Engelsman/Amerikaan

I don't understand
Ik begrijp het niet

Please speak more slowly
Kunt u langzamer praten, alstublieft

Can you help me?
Kunt u mij helpen?

Where is...? *Waar is...?*

I'm sorry (or excuse me)
Excuseer/Pardon

What time is it?
Hoe laat is het?

yes *ja*

no *neen*

please *alstublieft*

thank you *dank u*

...(very much) *...(wel)*

hello *hallo*

goodbye *tot ziens*

good evening *Goeden avond*

tomorrow *morgen*

this morning *vanmorgen*

this afternoon

Above: while most people speak English, most signage is in Dutch.

deze namiddag

this evening *vanavond*

Shopping

Where is the nearest...
Waar is de...

...bank?
...dichtstbijzijnde?

...post office?
...postkantoor?

Do you take credit cards?
Neemt u crediet kaarten?

Have you got? *Hebt u...?*

Anything else? *Iets anders?*

enough *genoeg*

too much *te veel*

chemist *de apotheek*

bakery *de bakkerij*

grocery *de kruidenier*

tobacconist *de tabakwinkel*

market *de markt*

Sightseeing

town *de stad*

old town *de oude stad*

cathedral *de kathedraal*

church *de kerk*

walk *de tour*

art gallery *de galerie*

tourist information office
het bureau voor toerisme (VVV)

free *gratis*

open *open*

closed *gesloten*

Emergencies

Help! *Help!*

Call a doctor/the police
Bel een dokter/de politie

Call an ambulance/the fire brigade
Bel een ziekenwagen/de brandweer

Where is the nearest telephone/hospital?
Waar is de dichtstbijzijnde telefoon/ziekenhuis?

I am sick
Ik ben ziek

I have lost my passport/purse
Ik ben mijn paspoort/ portemonnee kwijt

Left: trying out speaking in Dutch is always appreciated.

coffee *koffie*
...with milk or cream
...met melk of room
...decaffeinated *...decafeine*
...black *...zwart*
filtered *filterkoffie*
cold *koud*
fizzy lemonade *limonade*
orange juice *sinaasappelsap*
fresh *vers*
hot chocolate *warme chocolade melk*
house wine *huiswijn*
pitcher *karaf*
wine *wijn*
red *rood*
white *wit*
sparkling wine *schuimwijn*
tea *thee*
...herb infusion
...kruidenthee
...camomile *...kamille*

Eating Out

breakfast *het ontbijt*
lunch *lunch/middageten*
dinner *diner/avondeten*
wine list *de wijnkaart*
the bill *de rekening*
I am a vegetarian
Ik ben vegetarier
I'd like to order
Ik wil bestellen
That is not what I ordered
Dit is niet wat ik besteld heb
Is service included?
Is de dienst inbegrepen?
to book
reserveren/boeken

Food and drink

butter *boter*
bread *brood*
rolls *broodjes*
eggs *eieren*
...with bacon...*met spek*
...with ham...*met ham*
cheese *kaas*
jam *confitur*
pancake *pannekoek*
yoghurt *joghurt*
salt *zout*
sugar *suiker*
meat *vlees*
steak *biefstuk*
kebab *brochette*
duck *eend*
well done *goedgebakken*

ham *ham*
veal *kalfsvlees*
turkey *kalkoen*
chicken *kip*
lamb *lamsvlees*
small pieces of bacon *spek*
pork *varkensvlees*
fish *vis*
herring *haring*
mussels *mosselen*
eel *paling*
tuna *tonijn*
seafood *zeevruchten*
fruit *vruchten*
vegetables *groenten*
potato *aardappel*
onion *ajuin/ui*
turnip *biet*
mushroom *champignon*
crisps/potato chips
dooierzwam
peas *erwten*
chips/french fries *frieten*
green salad *groene sla*
lentils *linzen*
garlic *look*
raw *rauw*
rice *rijst*
tomato *tomaat*
cake *gebak/taart*
whipped cream *slagroom*
drinks *dranken*
beer *bier*
...bottled *...een fles*
...on tap *...van het vat*

Consonants

As a rule, the 'hard consonants' such as **t**, **k**, **s** and **p** are pronounced almost the same as in English, but sometimes a little softer. For example, the Dutch would refer to little as *'liddle'*.

j is pronounced as 'y' (meaning *ja* (yes) is pronounced *ya*)
v is pronounced as 'f' (meaning *vis* (fish) is pronounced *fiss*)
je is pronounced as 'yer'
tje is pronounced as 'ch' (meaning *botje* 'little bone' is pronounced *botchyer*)

Vowels

ee is pronounced as 'ay' (meaning *nee* (no) is pronounced as *nay*)
oo is pronounced as 'oh' (meaning *hoop* (hope) is pronounced as *hope*)
ij is pronounced as 'eay' (meaning *ijs* (ice cream) is pronounced *ace*)
a is pronounced as 'u' (meaning *bank* (bank) is pronounced as *bunk*).

Literature

The number and variety of bookshops in Amsterdam is testimony to the bookishness of its inhabitants. Included in the listings below is a selection of those that stock titles in English, though if you are a student of Dutch (or are content to look at the pictures), your choice includes specialist outlets for comics, antiquarian tomes, gay and lesbian interest, art and architecture, religious and new-age books. There is also an open-air book market held every Friday (10am–6pm) on Spui in the city's Old Centre. Meanwhile, for those looking to widen their breadth of experience of Dutch literature, see the reading list below.

The Dutch Literary Scene

Given the appetite of Amsterdam's inhabitants for culture and debate, it is perhaps surprising that so few of its authors are widely read outside the Netherlands. The 'Great Three' of Dutch post-war literature – **Willem Hermans**, **Harry Mulisch** and **Gerard Reve** – together with addition of **Jan Wolkers**, are undoubtedly worthy of greater attention from translators and publishers.

Moving in the other direction, English and American literature has wide currency in Amsterdam, with plenty of exposure in bookshops as well as at numerous literary events. The **John Adams Institute for American Literature** (tel: 020 624 7280; www.john-adams.nl), for example, offers a series of readings throughout the year at various venues in the city. Authors who have participated include **John Irving**, **Paul Theroux**, **Peter Matthiessen** and **Carol Shields**. Bookshops such as the American Book Center,

Athenaeum and Scheltema *(see right)* also hold regular lectures, signings and other events.

Further Reading

LITERATURE

Love in Amsterdam (1962)
Freeling, Nicolas
Detective novels featuring maverick cop Van der Valk.

Beyond Sleep (1966)
Hermans, Willem Frederik
One of the greatest modern Dutch novels.

The Assault (1982)
Mulisch, Harry
World War II story set in Amsterdam (also made into a classic film).

Rituals (1980)
Nooteboom, Cees
The most famous of Nooteboom's novels and almost entirely set in Amsterdam.

Parents Worry (1990)
Reve, Gerard
Novel about sex, booze and religion. Excellent.

Turkish Delight (1969)
Wolkers, Jan
Famous novel – also made into a film by **Paul Verhoeven**.

Held in May each year, the **Amsterdam Literary Festival** (www.amsterdamliterary festival.com) celebrates international writing by organising a series of events, most of which are conducted in English. Famous novelists, historians, journalists and poets are invited to give lectures, readings, workshops and book-signings.

HISTORY AND CULTURE

The Diary of a Young Girl (1952)
Frank, Anne
Few books have been as widely read as the diary of Anne Frank.

Dutch Painting (1978)
Fuchs, R.H.
Thames and Hudson paperback offering a concise and intelligent overview of Dutch painting from the Middle Ages to the present.

Amsterdam – A Brief Life in the City (1999)
Mak, Geert
Traces the city's progress from a little town of merchants and fishermen into a thriving metropolis.

Left: the esoteric and well-stocked Athenaeum.

626 6266; Mon–Sat 10am–6pm, Sun 11.30am–4pm; Tram: 4, 9, 14; map p.136 B3
Shop selling second-hand English-language books, with particular strength in literature and social sciences.

Pied-à-Terre
Overtoom 135–137; tel: 020 612 2314; www.piedaterre.nl; Mon 1–6pm, Tue, Wed, Fri 10am–6pm, Thur until 9pm, Sat until 5pm; Tram: 1, 2, 5; map p.133 C3
Travel books, guides and maps.

Scheltema
Koningsplein 20; tel: 020 523 1411; Mon–Wed and Fri–Sat 10am–6pm, Thur until 9pm, Sun noon–6pm; Tram: 1, 2, 5; map p.136 A4
Reputedly Amsterdam's largest bookshop. Stocks many English books and has a good remaindered-book section.

Waterstones
Kalverstraat 152; tel: 020 638 3821; www.waterstones.co.uk; Mon 10am–6pm, Tue, Wed, Fri 9.30am–7pm; Thur until 9pm, Sat 10am–6.30pm, Sun 11am–6pm; Tram: 1, 2, 4, 5, 9, 14, 16, 24, 25; map p.136 A3
English-language bookshop.

The Dutch Revolt (1988)
Parker, Geoffrey
Vivid history of the Dutch revolt against the Spanish during the Eighty Years War (1568–1648).
Dutch Art and Architecture 1600–1800 (1988)
Rosenberg et al
Standard work, first published in 1966, and since rewritten by popular demand. Illustrated in black and white.
The Embarrassment of Riches (1988)
Schama, Simon
Academic yet readable examination of culture and society during Holland's Golden Age.
The Low Sky: Understanding the Dutch (1996)
Van der Horst, Han
Explores modern Holland's dilemmas, paradoxes and taboos.

Bookshops

American Book Center
Spui 12; tel: 020 625 5537; www.abc.nl; Mon–Wed, Fri–Sat 10am–8pm, Thur until 9pm, Sun 11am–6.30pm; Tram: 1, 2, 4, 5, 9, 14, 16, 24, 25; map p.136 A3
News centre and bookshop that stocks English-language books and magazines as well as staging a variety of events.

Athenaeum Nieuwscentrum
Spui 14–16; tel: 020 514 1460; www.athenaeum.nl; Mon–Wed, Fri–Sat 8am–8pm, Thur until 9pm, Sun 10am–6pm; Tram: 1, 2, 5; map p.136 A3
News centre and bookshop that stocks journals and books from all over the world.

Book Exchange
Kloveniersburgwal 58; tel: 020

Right: the quirky Book Exchange.

Markets

Amsterdam's markets are wonderful. Perhaps not in the way that those of Paris set your mouth watering, but because they show the varied face of this city, and may tempt visitors out into some of the more interesting areas away from the tourist trails in the centre. The food markets show the increasing multiracial face of the city, with stalls devoted to unusual produce from places like Indonesia and Surinam. You'll find there's more to Dutch cheese than just Edam and Gouda, and in the clothes markets there are unusual Dutch fashion styles to be found in among the bargains.

City Centre

Oudemanhuis Book Market

Oudemanhuispoort; Mon–Fri 11am–4pm; Tram: 4, 9, 14; map p.136 B3

Book-lovers should make for this little side street in the university area, where there's a covered book market on weekdays. It's been here since the 18th century, catering to the university's scholars, but the contents of the stalls are by no means all highbrow. There's sheet music too, and it's the place where you might find an atmospheric old print of Amsterdam, well worth taking home and framing.

Postzegelmarkt

Nieuwezijds Voorburgwal; Wed, Sun 11am–4pm; Tram: 1, 2, 5; map p.136 A2

Along Nieuwezijds Voorburgwal, behind the Royal Palace on Dam Square, is this specialist market which is mainly for stamp and coin collectors, although you'll also find coins, postcards and medals too. It attracts buyers and sellers from all over the Netherlands.

Western Canal Belt and the Jordaan

Boerenmarkt

Westerstraat/Noorderkerkstraat; Sat 9am–3pm; Tram: 3, 10; map p.130 B3

This is one of the biggest organic farmers' markets in the Netherlands, and getting bigger every year as more people turn to organic foods and other goods. There are stalls selling meat, fish, vegetables, fruit, herbs, cheeses, wine, chocolates and other sweets, and there's often street entertainment too. Some stalls sell candles, oils and other similar items.

Looier Arts and Antiques Market

Elandsgracht 109; tel: 020 624 9038; www.looier.nl; Sat–Thur

> Opening times for markets are only approximate. The days don't usually change, but the opening and closing times might vary from time to time depending on the weather, and how business is doing. And it's always best to get there early to get the best produce or bargains.

11am–5pm; Tram: 7, 10, 17; map p.133 D1

This is one of the more serious antiques and collectors' markets in the city, with some highly priced goods on offer. If you're hoping for a bargain then you'll need to know what you're looking for, but bargain or not, there are some quality items on the 72 stalls here: mirrors, paintings, jewellery, furniture, dolls, ceramics, glassware and many more.

Noordermarkt

Noordermarkt; Mon 8am–1pm; Tram: 3, 10; map p.130 B3

The Noordermarkt is the market for bargain-hunters, especially if you like to find cheap clothes, as there's a fine collection of clothes stalls in among the other flea market stalls.

Rommelmarkt

Looiersgracht 38; daily 11am–5pm; Tram: 7, 10, 17; map p.133 D1

In the south of the Jordaan is the daily Rommelmarkt flea market, selling anything and everything from clothes and books to toys, kitchenware, CDs, old vinyl albums and even some antiques.

Left: buy seeds to grow your own tulips at Bloemenmarkt.

discovered by travel magazines and TV channels. It even has its own website and newspaper. As well as food, it's very good for clothes, with lots of fun items that are junky but funky, and there's often music or other events going on.

Waterlooplein Market

Waterlooplein; Mon–Sat 9am–5pm; Metro: Waterlooplein; map p.137 C4

Being so central and close to the Rembrandthuis and other tourist attractions, the Waterlooplein flea market is very well known now, and prices have risen accordingly. It's a colourful place, though, by the water, and with plenty of stalls to browse through, including clothes, antiques and general junk.

De Pijp

Albert Cuypmarkt

Albert Cuypstraat; Mon–Sat 9am–5pm; Tram: 4, 16, 24; map p.133 E4

This is one of the best food markets in the city, being in the multi-ethnic Pijp neighbourhood and having to cater daily (except Sunday) to the local food shoppers. There are also plenty of stalls selling clothes, junk, domestic stuff, cosmetics, jewellery and loads more besides.

Left: inexpensive clothes at the Albert Cuypmarkt.

ful flower market. This is a big magnet for tourists, especially when there are abundant displays of Dutch tulips to be photographed, but it's also much used by local people, who like to have flowers in their homes. You can also buy seeds, seedlings and bulbs here too. Some stalls also open here on a Sunday, but not as many as on the other days of the week.

Jodenbuurt, the Plantage and the Oost

Dappermarkt

Dapperstraat; www.dappermarkt.nl; Mon–Sat 9am–5pm; Tram: 3, 6, 10; map p.135 D3

Because it's out in the east of the city, prices are lower than at the markets closer in, so another good place for the bargain-hunter. It may not stay that way for long, though, as it's been voted best street market in the Netherlands and has been

Right: investigating antiques at the Waterlooplein Market.

Westermarkt

Westerstraat; Mon 9am–1pm; Tram: 3, 10; map p.130 B3

The Westermarkt is another junky market – or bric-a-brac if you prefer. It's known to be good for clothes and fabrics, and you'll also find shoes, watches, jewellery and a whole range of domestic stuff, often from bankrupt stock.

Southern Canal Belt and Leidseplein

Bloemenmarkt

On the Singel canal, between Koningsplein and Muntplein; Mon–Sat 8.30am–5pm; Tram: 1, 2, 4; map p.136 A4

The best-known market in the city is undoubtedly the colour-

Museums and Galleries

In Amsterdam, it seems that anyone with an enthusiasm, whether for trams or tattoos, opens a museum. There are some big ones here too, of course, celebrating the best of Dutch art. The Rijksmuseum has the world's most important collection of art from the Golden Age, including many works by Rembrandt. Meanwhile, the Van Gogh Museum is the world's largest collection of his work. Both museums are unmissable, but the others are up to you; whatever your interests, you are likely to find a museum celebrating them.

City Centre

Allard Pierson Museum

Oude Turfmarkt 127; tel: 020 525 2556; www.allardpierson museum.nl; Tue–Fri 10am–5pm, Sat 1–5pm; admission charge; Tram: 4, 9, 14; map p.136 B4

This archaeological museum is run by the University of Amsterdam, and is the city's prime collection of items from the civilisations of the ancient Greeks, Egyptians, the Romans and the Etrurians, Cyprus and the Near East (which is what archaeologists like to call the Middle East). The items range from about

---

Amsterdam's Best Museums
If time is limited and you want to focus on the city's best museums, then these are the ones to go for.
Art:
Rijksmuseum *(p.85)*
Van Gogh Museum *(p.85)*
History
Amsterdams Historisch Museum *(see right)*
Anne Frank Huis *(p.80)*
Verzetsmuseum *(p.88)*
Science:
NEMO *(p.89)*

4000 BC to AD 500, and from the touching everyday objects such as bronze mirrors and children's toys to everyone's fascination: mummies. Unfortunately the labelling is mostly in Dutch, though there are some English captions, and some of the display cases are starting to acquire an archaeological interest of their own, but the collections themselves are certainly impressive.

Amsterdams Historisch Museum

Nieuwezijds Voorburgwal 357/Kalverstraat 92; tel: 020 523 1822; www.ahm.nl; Tram: 1, 2, 4; Mon–Fri 10am–5pm, Sat–Sun 11am–5pm; admission charge; map p.136 A3

If you want to leave Amsterdam with a deeper understanding of this intriguing city, then the Historic Museum is where you will find it. It is also a fascinating and fun place, just like the city it celebrates. It sprawls around a collection of 17th-century houses, and is a place where history really comes alive, prompting you to look at Amsterdam's

streets, canals and people in a different light when you emerge. Don't miss Cornelius Anthonizoon's fascinating 1538 painting showing a bird's-eye view of Amsterdam, and link this with the computer-generated map of the city showing how Amsterdam has grown over the years. If you want to learn about Amsterdam's first lesbian bar, that's here too, as is the machine that was used to rescue horses from the canals. Combine these with heart-rending displays on the dark days of World War II, and then countless personal items and photos of Amsterdammers over the years, and you have a museum that shouldn't be missed.

Sexmuseum Venustempel

Damrak 18; tel: 020 622 8376; www.sexmuseumamsterdam.nl; daily 9.30am–11.30pm; admission charge; Metro: Centraal Station; map p.130 C4

Amsterdam has two museums devoted to the erotic arts, and this is the more commercial one on the busy Damrak. It spreads itself over three floors and has display

Left: Van Gogh's *Bedroom in Arles* at the Van Gogh Museum *(see p.85).*

tel: 020 623 5961; www.hash museum.com; daily 10am–10pm; admission charge; Metro: Nieuwmarkt; map p.136 B2

It's almost inevitable that Amsterdam would have a museum devoted to weed, and that the museum should have its own coffeeshop and an adjacent Seed Bank where you can buy their equivalent of museum repro-ductions. In fact the museum itself isn't that large, and more of a curiosity, its most interesting displays being about the medicinal value of smoking cannabis. There's information, too, about the turning of hemp into paper and textiles, and the museum also has displays behind glass of the different types of marijuana-growing.

areas with names like the **Casanova Gallery**, **Fanny Hill Street** and the **Marquis de Sade Hall**. It's actually quite a bright and cheerful place, not sleazy and shady, and unless you're already an aficionado of the erotic arts some of the exhibits are defi-nite eye-openers. After a while you even start to look at the fire extinguishers and wonder if they are some bizarre sexual implement. It's not to everyone's taste, but it is inexpensive and definitely gives value for money.

mock-up of a prostitute's window, showing what's behind the scenes, man-nequins wearing provocative costumes through the ages, Indian erotic carvings and adult cartoons like a raunchy version of *Snow White and the Seven Dwarves*. By far the most interesting exhibits are some of John Lennon's erotic drawings, and a non-erotic sketch of his famous bed-in for peace with Yoko Ono in the Amsterdam Hilton.

Museum Amstelkring
Oudezijds Voorburgwal 40; tel: 020 624 6604; www.museum amstelkring.nl; Mon–Sat 10am–5pm, Sun 1–5pm; admission charge; Tram: 4, 9, 14; map p.136 C1

The Amstelkring is one of Amsterdam's little gems. It couldn't be more of a con-trast to the Red Light District that surrounds it, and even

Nieuwmarkt and the Red Light District

Erotic Museum
Oudezijds Achterburgwal 54; tel: 020 624 7303; Sun–Thur 11am–1am, Fri–Sat 11am–2am; admission charge; Metro: Nieuwmarkt; map p.136 C2

Based in Amsterdam's Red Light District, the Erotic Museum is more blatantly sexual while the Sex Museum *(see left)* is more about erot-ica. This is what you might expect from a sex museum in the Red Light District – pretty full-frontal. Exhibits include a

The Hash, Marihuana and Hemp Museum
Oudezijds Achterburgwal 130;

Below: the Amsterdams Historisch Museum.

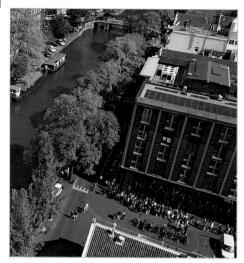

Left: there is often a long queue for the Anne Frank Huis *(top)*; *(middle)* the entrance to the secret annexe where Anne Frank *(bottom)* and her family hid.

warren of a house you get a real feeling of what life was like in Amsterdam in the 17th century.

Western Canal Belt and the Jordaan

Anne Frank Huis

Prinsengracht 267; tel: 020 556 7100; www.annefrank.org; mid-Mar to mid-Sept: Sun–Fri 9am–9pm, Sat 9am–10pm, July–Aug: daily 9am–10pm, mid-Sept to mid-Mar: daily 9am–7pm; admission charge; Tram: 13, 17; map p.130 B4

Although most people know the Anne Frank story before they get here, nothing can prepare you for the shock and the emotions that the reality stirs up. It brings the overwhelming story of the shock of the Holocaust down to the individual tale of one family, and in particular one young girl. Apart from the addition of some visitor facilities, the house is much as it was when the Frank family went into hiding here. To see the rooms where they lived and hid from the Nazis is to realise what they endured, only to be betrayed at the end with the inevitable consequences. The additions to the building include a wing where there are displays not just about the persecution of the Jews, but about all persecutions of peoples around the world. Few people can emerge from the visit unaffected in some way.

Bijbels Museum

Herengracht 366–368; tel: 020 624 2436; www.bijbelsmuseum.nl; Mon–Sat 10am–5pm, Sun 11am–5pm;

if it wasn't here its secret would still surprise. Hidden at the top of this 17th-century house is an attic church, which was added to it in 1663. This was after the Reformation (known here as the Alteration), when Catholics in Amsterdam were forbidden from practising their religion in public, and had to do so furtively. The size of the chapel is surprising, as it seats 150 people, and on the way up to it through the rest of this

admission charge; Tram: 1, 2, 5; map p.133 E1

In a city notorious for sex and drugs, its other more historic and cultural delights can come as a surprise. A Biblical Museum may sound less than thrilling to most people, but it's an enjoyable place because it deals with its subject in a broader context. Yes there are many examples of Bibles on display, and beautiful objects they are too, but there are many other items to see. The best are the examples of Dutch model-making, as it became fashionable here in the late 19th century to make and collect models of biblical scenes. There are models of the temples of Solomon and Herod, designed from information in biblical texts, and a stunning model of the Tabernacle, which housed the Ark of the Covenant. There are archaeological finds from the biblical period too, all displayed in two delightful 17th-century houses by the Herengracht canal.

Felix Meritis Cultural Centre

Keizersgracht 324; tel: 020 626 2321; www.felix.meritis.nl; Mon–Fri 9am–end of last performance, Sat–Sun open for performances only; admission charge; Tram: 1, 2, 5; map p.133 D1

This is the Felix Meritis European Centre for Arts, Culture and Science, to give it its full grand title, and it was founded in 1789 by the rich and cultured citizens of Amsterdam. It is still based in the same building, which was recently well restored, and today it hosts conferences and debates, music concerts and exhibitions of art, photography and other media.

Even if there is nothing in particular you want to see, the building itself is worth visiting for a sense of late 18th-century Dutch grandeur.

Huis Marseille Museum for Photography

Keizersgracht 401; tel: 020 531 8989; www.huismarseille.nl; Tue–Sun 11am–6pm; admission charge; Tram: 1, 2, 5; map p.133 E2

This photographic museum is based in a canal house and provides five large gallery rooms where there always seems to be something unusual on display. The work range from ultra-modern challenging works to more traditional forms, like collections of historical daguerreotypes. There's a film and video collection too, and a library, with photographic books for sale and catalogues from past exhibitions.

Stedelijk Museum Bureau Amsterdam

Rozenstraat 59; tel: 020 422 0471; www.smba.nl; Tue–Sun 11am–5pm during exhibitions; free; Tram: 13, 14, 17; map p.133 D1

This offshoot of the Stedelijk Museum of Modern Art acts as a smaller gallery for temporary and contemporary exhibitions by up-and-coming

The Anne Frank House is one of the biggest visitor attractions in Amsterdam, drawing almost a million people a year. It is also quite small, and visitors must file up the stairs and through the rooms, which can take time. Queues inevitably build up as the day goes on, so to avoid too long a wait it is best to make the effort and join the people who start queuing up to half an hour before it opens. Either that or wait until the end of the day in the summer months, and visit when most people are eating dinner.

new artists from or based in Amsterdam. The work tends to be pretty avant-garde, and in a liberal city like Amsterdam that can mean very challenging indeed. It includes all kinds of art – painting, photography, video, kinetic and computer art.

Woonbootmuseum (Houseboat Museum)

Prinsengracht, opposite 296; tel: 020 427 0750; www.houseboat museum.nl; Mar–Oct Tue–Sun 11am–5pm, Nov–Feb Fri–Sun 11am–5pm; admission charge; Tram: 13, 14, 17; map p.133 D1

This charming little attraction isn't a collection of houseboats but is a museum on a

Right: the Woonbootmuseum.

81

houseboat, the *Hendrika Maria*, whose displays show what it was and is like to live on an Amsterdam houseboat. It is surprisingly spacious, and although it's no longer occupied it was someone's home for about 20 years, complete with central heating, hot showers, and a living room that's as big as in many a regular house. For a modest admission fee, this little glimpse into the way many Amsterdammers still live is well worth it.

Southern Canal Belt and Leidseplein

De Appel
Nieuwe Spiegelstraat 10; tel: 020 625 5651; www.deappel.nl; Tue–Sun 11am–6pm; admission charge; Tram: 1, 2, 5; map p.133 E2
De Appel is one of the most enjoyable of Amsterdam's many modern art galleries and exhibition spaces. It embraces every art form, including painting, photography, video and installation art, and a lot of the exhibitions – which usually change every few weeks – are welcomingly unpretentious, and often fun. There's also free admission on the first Sunday of each month.

Right: the grand garden and displays at the fascinating Museum Van Loon.

Kattenkabinet
Herengracht 497; tel: 020 626 5378; www.kattenkabinet.nl; Tue–Fri 10am–4pm, Sat–Sun noon–5pm; admission charge; Tram: 1, 4, 9; map p.133 E2
The Cat Cabinet is yet another of Amsterdam's offbeat but enjoyable museums. If you think it sounds far too cutesy an idea, think again. Cats are what hold the collection together, but it shows how our feline friends have influenced artists over the years. These aren't just the cats of the homely birthday card, but are cats that have inspired Picasso, been featured in works by Toulouse-Lautrec, and are behind some rather scary works like the *Cat Witch of Okaba* by Japanese artist Utagawa Kuniyoshi. The more familiar side can be seen in photos of Truman Capote holding a cat and paintings by Sal Meijer, a Jewish artist from Amsterdam who produced some memorable cat paintings among his portraits of everyday Amsterdam life.

Max Euwe Centrum
Max Euweplein 30a; tel: 020 625 7017; www.maxeuwe.nl; Tue–Fri noon–4pm; free; Tram: 1, 2, 5; map p.133 D3
Max Euwe may not be a well-known name these days, but he is the only chess world champion that the Netherlands has produced. It's a nation more associated with Old Masters than Grandmasters, but Max Euwe was champion of the chess world from 1935–7, and was also known in his native country as a mathematician and a respected writer of books about chess. In this chess centre that stands in his memory, there's an exhibition on the history of chess, historic chess sets, a library, portraits of the Dutch chess greats and the chance to use some of the collection of computerised chess machines, or perhaps play against a human being using the giant chess set outside.

Pijpenkabinet
Prinsengracht 488; tel: 020 421 1779; www.pijpenkabinet.nl; Wed–Sat noon–6pm; admission charge; Tram: 1, 2, 5; map p.133 E2
A Pipe Museum? Why not. There's every other kind of museum in Amsterdam. The collection was begun by Don Duco in 1969, when he acquired some ancient pipes

that had been found during archaeological works in the city. This led to an interest in how far back pipes were smoked, and on how they developed over the centuries in different cultures around the world. The result of that initial curiosity is now the National Pipe Collection, containing over 20,000 items on display in a handsome house that was built on the Prinsengracht in about 1700. The oldest pipes on display are about 4,000 years old, and were found in a burial tomb in Laos. There are also pipes of peace used by Native Americans, royal pipes, finely carved meerschaum pipes and the longest pipe in the world!

Eastern Canal Belt and Rembrandtplein

Foam

Keizersgracht 609; tel: 020 551 6500; www.foam.nl; Sat–Wed 10am–6pm, Thur–Fri 10am–9pm; admission charge; Tram: 16, 24, 25; map p.133 E2

Foam is only a small photographic gallery but it's a very influential one, publishing its own magazine as well as limited-edition prints, and it acts as a meeting point for the city's creative photographers. The galleries are light and bright and the exhibitions, which change every couple of months, feature both international names and home-grown Dutch talent that the gallery owners feel is worth a showcase.

Museum van Loon

Keizersgracht 672; tel: 020 624 5255; www.museumvanloon.nl; Wed–Mon 11am–5pm; admission charge; Tram: 16, 24, 25; map p.133 E2

The first person to live in this house when it was built in 1672 was Ferdinand Bol, a pupil of Rembrandt who went on to become a renowned Dutch artist in his own right. In the 19th century the house was bought by the van Loon family, who co-founded the

Dutch East India Company. The family naturally became hugely wealthy, and it is their sumptuous collection of furniture, paintings, porcelain, silver and other valuable items that make up this fine arts museum. The interior of the house has been restored to show how it was in the 18th century, and you can also visit the garden. This is something of a surprise, as it's much larger than you might think possible in Amsterdam. The museum is worth visiting for this alone, a glimpse behind the frontages of one of those tall canal houses.

Museum Willet-Holthuysen

Herengracht 605; tel: 020 523 1822; www.museumwillet holthuysen.nl; Mon–Fri 10am–5pm, Sat–Sun 11am–5pm; admission charge; Tram: 4, 9, 14; map p.134 A2

The Willet-Holthuysen family made their money from the coal industry, and spent a lot of it furnishing this house which they bought in the 1850s. The house itself goes back to 1685, but the main style chosen for the décor was the flamboyant 18th-century Louis XVI, as popular in Amsterdam as elsewhere. The house was left to the city

Left: an exhibition at Foam.

Right: the Rijksmuseum dominates Museumplein.

Right: the Rijksmuseum dominates Museumplein.

by the family in 1895, on condition that it be opened as a museum, and it has remained open to this day. It is now the only house of this kind in Amsterdam that has its original furnishings and is permanently open to the public, and you also have the chance to see its garden, otherwise hidden from view. It's a private peek into a patrician lifestyle.

Reflex Galleries

Weteringhans 79a and 83; tel: 020 627 2832; www.reflex-art.nl; Tue–Sat 11am–6pm; free; Tram: 7, 10; map p.133 E3

The two Reflex Galleries are among the best and most successful commercial modern art galleries in the city. They put on art and photography exhibitions by some high-profile names like Jeff Koons and Willem de Kooning, and they publish books too. There are two galleries opposite each other on the same street (the **Reflex Modern Art Gallery** is at number 79a, and the **Reflex New Art Gallery** at number 83), and there's sure to be something of interest on at one if not both of them.

Tassenmuseum Hendrikje

Herengracht 573; tel: 020 524 6452; www.tassenmuseum.nl; daily 10am–5pm; admission charge; Tram: 4, 9; map p.134 A2

With over 3,500 bags and purses in its collection, the Museum of Bags and Purses is the largest museum of its kind in the world. As with many other of Amsterdam's specialist museums, you may enter mildly curious but quickly become fascinated by the history of the handbag. The collection covers the Middle Ages to modern times – they even have one of Madonna's handbags. All the famous designer names are represented, with work by the likes of Gucci, Versace, Chanel, Dolce & Gabbana, Donna Karan and Alexander McQueen. There are bags covered in feathers, made of suede, of metal and of snakeskin. There's a pleasant café, and the whole collection is housed in a mansion that was built in the 1660s.

The Museum Quarter, Vondelpark and the South

Electrische Museumtramlijn Amsterdam

Amstelveenseweg 264; tel: 020 673 7538; www.museumtram.nl; Apr–Oct: Sun 11am–5pm, July–Aug: Wed (check for times); admission charge; Tram: 16

The opening hours are limited here but if you want to see, and especially ride on, an old tram then you should plan your visit carefully. The ride is a real delight, lasting an hour or so and taking you out through the lovely Amsterdamse Bos park area to the south of the city.

Below: an old tram at the Electrische Museumtramlijn.

Back at base, which is a little way out of the centre, south of the southern end of the Vondelpark, there's a collection of old trams from Amsterdam and elsewhere. Tram rides run about every 30 minutes, and there's no need to book ahead.

House of Bols
Paulus Potterstraat 14; tel: 020 570 8575; www.houseofbols.nl; Wed–Sun noon–6pm; admission charge; Tram: 2, 3, 5; map p.133 D3
If you want a change from art after visiting the Rijksmuseum and the Van Gogh Museum, right by is this place devoted to the art of making Dutch *jenever* gin. It's housed over two floors of the Amsterdam HQ of the Bols company, whose history goes back to 1575. Naturally there's a strong focus on the Bols brand, but it is an enjoyable look at the making of *jenever*, and of cocktails generally – you can even try your hand at being a bartender, but if you don't want to mix it you can just drink it.

Rijksmuseum
Stadhouderskade 42; tel: 020 674 7047; www.rijksmuseum.nl; daily 9am–6pm, Fri until 8.30pm; admission charge; Tram: 2, 5, 6; map p.133 E3
The most important art museum in the Netherlands has been closed for several years for very extensive renovation work, and at the time of writing is not scheduled to reopen fully until 2013 at the earliest. Until then only the highlights of its collection of over 7 million items are on display, but what highlights they are. There are over 400 of the museum's most important paintings and other items, including significant

works by its most popular artists, Rembrandt and Vermeer. Rembrandt's monumental work *The Night Watch* is given pride of place in the already refurbished Philips Wing along with other works from the Dutch Golden Age including Frans Hals, Jan Steen and Jan Vermeer. There's also a large selection of exquisite Delftware on show, along with silverware and other objets d'art.

Stedelijk Musuem of Modern Art
Paulus Potterstraat 13; tel: 020 573 2911; www.stedelijk.nl; Closed for refurbishment until 2009; Tram: 2, 5, 6; map p.133 D3
Like the modern art it displays, the Stedelijk Museum has not been standing still. While its main building here by the Van Gogh Museum is being renovated, the collection has been on the move. After being housed until recently in the former post office, the Post CS-Building close to Centraal Station, there are going to be displays from the museum's collection in various places around the city, including the Nieuwe Kerk (*see Churches and Synagogues, p.38*) and the Van Gogh Museum (*see right*). Contemporary art and

As well as looking at these listings for museums and galleries, it's worth investigating the city's churches (*see p.38–9*), as several of these are now major exhibition spaces, notably the Nieuwe Kerk and the Oude Kerk.

some mobile exhibitions are likely to pop up anywhere. The Stedelijk has been amassing modern art since it opened in 1895, and its collection includes work by Picasso, Malevich, Matisse and Chagall, and more modern names including Warhol, De Kooning and Rauschenberg. It's especially interesting as, in addition to the iconic works, it includes a lot of the featured artists' lesser-known works, as well as contemporary video and kinetic art. Some of these touring exhibitions are scheduled to go on until December 2009, so watch out for details of when the main building might be re-opening.

Van Gogh Museum
Paulus Potterstraat 7; tel: 020 570 5200; www.vangogh museum.com; daily 10am–6pm, Fri until 10pm; admission charge; Tram: 2, 3, 5; map p.133 D3
One good thing about the Rijksmuseum's collection

Right: the Rijksmuseum is packed with the Old Masters.

Left: the famous *Sunflowers*, at the Van Gogh Museum.

Museum in St Petersburg does not retain its own core collection but does put on changing exhibitions from the vast Hermitage collection. It's always worth checking what's on here while you're in Amsterdam, as some of the items put on display are quite remarkable. Recent exhibitions have covered German Romantic landscape paintings, Greek gold, an exhibition on the lives of the last Tsar and Tsarina, Nicholas and Alexandra, and pilgrim treasures from Byzantium and Jerusalem.

Joods Historisch Museum

Nieuwe Amstelstraat 1; tel: 020 531 0310; www.jhm.nl; daily 11am–5pm; admission charge; Metro: Waterlooplein; map p.137 D4

The story of Jewish culture in Amsterdam and throughout the Netherlands is told in the moving collections housed in four adjoining synagogues. The oldest of these, the Great Synagogue, was built in 1671 and is itself an indication of the strength of the Jewish population here before the tragedy of World War II. In 1730 the New Synagogue was dedicated, which became the fourth synagogue in the city. As well as the buildings themselves the museum has a collection of over 11,000 objects, though only a fraction of these can be put on display at any one time – paintings, photographs, documents and religious artefacts. There's also a separate **Children's**

being currently limited to the highlights is that it gives most visitors, with limited time in the city, a greater chance to spent more time in Amsterdam's other unmissable collection: the Van Gogh Museum. Here, too, you need to plan to arrive early to beat the crowds, but even if it takes a while to get in, the wait is worth it. The museum inside is very light and spacious, and can accommodate a fair amount of crowding.

What draws the crowds is the world's largest collection

of work by the man who is one of the world's most popular artists. Here there are over 200 of Van Gogh's paintings, almost 600 drawings, and large selections of his letters and notebooks. As well as some of his most famous works, like *Sunflowers*, *The Yellow House*, *Wheatfield with Crows* and *The Potato Eaters*, are some searing self-portraits, and works by artists who influenced him, including Gauguin and Toulouse-Lautrec.

There are also temporary exhibitions in an extension of the main building, sleekly designed by the Japanese architect Kisho Kurokawa.

Jodenbuurt, the Plantage and the Oost

Hermitage Amsterdam

Nieuwe Herengracht 14; tel: 020 530 8755; www.hermitage.nl; daily 10am–5pm; admission charge; Metro: Waterlooplein; map p.134 B2

The Amsterdam branch of the stunning Hermitage

A good time for art-lovers to visit Amsterdam is during the **Open Ateliers** event, when artists in the Jordaan open their studios for visitors to see them at work. It happens over a few days in either May or June each year, and dates and further information are available on the website, though at the moment only in Dutch: www.openateliersjordaan.nl.

Right: the Children's Museum at the Joods Historisch Museum and *(above right)* the on-site New Synagogue.

Right: fine arts at the Hermitage Amsterdam.

Museum, which introduces Jewish traditions to the kids in a fun way.

Rembrandthuis

Jodenbreestraat 4; tel: 020 520 0400; www.rembrandthuis.nl; daily 10am–5pm; admission charge; Metro: Nieuwmarkt; map p.137 C3

If the Rijksmuseum shows the public face of Rembrandt on a big scale (not least his colossal *Night Watch* canvas), then the house in which he lived and worked is the private face. Rembrandt Harmenszoon van Rijn (1609–69) was born in Leiden, but came to Amsterdam in 1631. Soon after arriving he took lodgings in Jodenbreestraat and in 1639 purchased this house. Unfortunately, his extravagant furnishings and running expenses contributed to his bankruptcy in 1656, when he was forced sell the house and many of his possessions. He was, nevertheless, allowed to stay in residence until 1658, at which time he made a new home in the Jordaan.

This house was opened as a museum in 1911, but

Right: fine arts at the Hermitage Amsterdam.

the interior of the building has been reconstructed as closely as possible to show what it was like at the time when Rembrandt lived there. It's a convincing re-creation of the mood of the house, including the artist's studio (where you may well find an artist working and displaying painting techniques), and his collection of artefacts from around the world, which fascinated him for their shapes and textures. There is also an extensive collection of his etchings.

In 1998, a new wing, adjacent to the house, was opened, housing 250 of the artist's drawings and etchings, as well as a

number of paintings. The extension has provided the opportunity to restore the house itself to as near its original state as possible.

87

Left: at the Tropical Museum.

more impressive inside with masses of stained glass. You don't even need to spend much time touring the museum if it doesn't appeal, but the visit is well worth the very modest admission price. SEE ALSO PALACES AND HOUSES, P.99

Verzetsmuseum
Plantage Kerklaan 61; tel: 020 620 2535; www.verzets museum.org; Tue–Fri 10am–5pm, Sat–Mon 11am–5pm; admission charge; Tram: 6, 9, 14; map p.134 C2

The Dutch Resistance Museum was recently chosen as the best museum in the Netherlands, and while you cannot compare it with the likes of the Rijksmuseum it tells this particular story incredibly well and power-fully. There are moving stories of bravery, and of collabor-ation too, and much of the information on display is from the first-hand accounts of people involved. There are also changing exhibitions, some showing how what happened in the 1940s still matters today. Anyone who has visited the **Anne Frank Huis** *(see p.80)* really should come here as well, to broaden the picture of what

Tropical Museum (Tropenmuseum)
Linnaeusstraat 2; tel: 020 568 8200; www.tropenmuseum.nl; daily 10am–5pm; admission charge; Tram: 9, 14; map p.135 D3

The Tropical Museum is well worth the short journey out to the east of the City Centre and not too far from the **Artis Zoo** *(see Children, p.36)*. Its very lively displays explore the cultures of the tropical areas of the world, expanding from its original coverage of those countries which were once part of the Dutch Empire. This ethnographic museum believes in using all the senses to help visitors understand the lives of other people, not just the visual approach of looking at dis-plays. There are a lot of world music concerts, for example, and the smells of Mumbai are made very real in an exhibition in the children's **Tropenmuseum Junior** also housed here. The topics cov-ered by exhibitions can be very lively too – voodoo was one recent example, and life in 1948 Palestine. SEE ALSO CHILDREN, P.36

Vakbondsmuseum
Henri Polaklaan 9; tel: 020 624 1166; www.deburcht.org; Tue–Fri 11am–5pm, Sun 1–5pm; admission charge; Tram: 6, 9, 14; map p.137 E4

A Trades Union Museum? You're on holiday, right? Well, the contents may not be everyone's idea of fun but it is worth visiting as it's a remarkable building. It was built in 1900 for the then-powerful Diamond Workers' Union, and designed by Hen-drik Petrus Berlage. Berlage is the Dutch architect who was also responsible for the **Beurs van Berlage** which bears his name. It's a striking and quite beautiful place from the outside, and even

Right: exhibits at the moving Verzetsmuseum.

Amsterdam, with its love of the quirky, has lots of specialist museums. In addition to some of the ones listed here, catering for people interested in cats, trams and pipes, there are several other museums devoted to what might be called minority interests. If you happen to be interested, though, then seek out the city's museums that tell the stories of pianolas, trade unions, tattoos, torture and journalism in the Netherlands, amongst other subjects.

was happening throughout the Netherlands to combat the Nazi occupation.

The Waterfront

National Maritime Museum (Scheepvaartmuseum)

Kattenburgerplein 1; tel: 020 523 2222; www.scheepvaart museum.nl; closed until 2010; Bus: 22, 23; Metro: Centraal Station; map p.134 C1

While this is temporarily closed for a major refurbishment, it will no doubt remain one of Amsterdam's most important museums when it reopens, currently scheduled for sometime in 2010. One of its major attractions, the *Amsterdam*, can still be seen nearby at the **NEMO** *(see right)*. The *Amsterdam* is a modern replica of an original East Indiaman, the ships that were used in the 17th–19th centuries to transport goods and people around the world. They were so successful that, although originally used by the Dutch, other countries soon started building them. By going aboard the *Amsterdam* you can see what life would have been like on those sea voyages which lasted

months, sometimes years.

At 350 years old, the building housing the Maritime Museum was in need of reconstruction and modernisation. It was originally a naval arsenal, and now tells the story of Dutch maritime history. There are some fascinating boats on display, from ice-breakers to royal barges and even a Greenpeace *Rainbow Warrior*. How the new museum displays these and its huge collection of maritime items will be very interesting to see.
SEE ALSO ARCHITECTURE, P.28

NEMO

Oosterdok 2; tel: 020 531 3233; www.e-nemo.nl; Tue–Sun 10am–5pm, daily during school holidays and June–Aug; admission charge; Metro: Centraal Station; map p.131 D4

Apart from the astonishing nature of the building itself, the five floors inside contain the largest science centre in the country. It's primarily aimed at children, and indeed opens longer during school holidays, but you don't need

to have a child with you to enjoy it – just a childlike curiosity and sense of fun. What happens when you kiss someone? Where do pimples come from? How do bridges and skyscrapers withstand high winds? What did a 1948 computer look like? All aspects of science are covered in an enjoyable hands-on way, with shows to attend and special events too.
SEE ALSO ARCHITECTURE, P.29

De Pijp

NINT Technologie Musuem

Tolstraat 129; tel: 020 570 8111; Mon–Fri 10am–5pm, Sat–Sun noon–5pm; map p.134 B4

With the emphasis on looking, playing and doing, this science and technology-focused museum's areas of specialisation include computers, electronics, telecommunications and optical illusions, making it a fascinating destination for kids and adults alike, especially if the weather takes a turn for the worse.

Right: children play on the DNA age machine at NEMO.

Music

A msterdam has a vibrant musical scene for its size. You may be hard-pressed to name any world-famous Amsterdam musicians, but the city has a superb range of concert venues and musicians, both resident and visiting. The quality runs across all genres too, from classical to metal. It's got some of the best and most innovative nightclubs in Europe *(see Nightlife, p.94–7)* and for 120 years has boasted one of the most acoustically perfect grand concert halls in the world. In between you'll find good jazz and blues venues, world music concerts, and visiting rock gods playing at venues like the Paradiso.

Classical Music

Just as rock stars like playing Amsterdam, so too do the great classical orchestras and musicians. It's partly to do with the excellent venues, and partly the appreciative audiences. Ticket prices are comparatively low here, and that creates broader audiences than elsewhere, and usually sell-out ones too. There isn't quite the same snob value, either, as you get in most European cities. Amsterdam is more democratic about its so-called 'high art', which

makes for a more relaxed evening out.

VENUES
Concertgebouw
Concertgebouwplein 2–6; tel: 020 671 8345/573 0511; www.concertgebouw.nl; box office: daily 10am–7pm, or later if there's a concert; phone bookings daily 10am–5pm; Tram: 2, 3, 5; map p.133 D4
Amsterdam's Concertgebouw is a concert hall in the grand classical European tradition. Busts of composers such as Bach and Beethoven gaze sternly down at the arriving

audience, and the imposing neoclassical facade of the building lets you know you are definitely there for a big night out. The hall opened in 1888 after five years of building work, and there are wooden piles sunk into the ground below it, supporting it in the way several important city buildings are supported.

The Concertgebouw has always been considered one of the most acoustically perfect concert halls in the world, and is the home of the Royal Concertgebouw Orchestra, the most important symphony orchestra in the Netherlands. There are two concert halls inside: the **Little Hall** *(Kleine Zaal)*, used for chamber concerts and smaller recitals, and the **Great Hall** *(Grote Zaal)*. Despite the high international standard of both the concerts and the acoustics, prices here are comparatively low – and there are even weekly free concerts in the Kleine Zaal, if you want to experience the building properly.

Left: the lit-up Muziekgebouw at night.

Left and below: the audience take their seats at Concertgebouw as the orchestra warms up.

clubs and theatres for artists who are breaking through, or the big names who just want to play a more intimate space occasionally, and as well as the more visible scene there's also still an underground scene, known just to locals. In many respects it's still the 1960s in Amsterdam.

It's the breadth of music in the city that also makes the place exciting, alongside the fact that it's so compact and most places are pretty easy to get to. From experimental electronic music to the earthiness of American blues, the thrash of heavy metal and the exuberance of some of the world music stars, it's all happening in Amsterdam, often all on the same night. The modern music fan should definitely check the listings magazines like *Amsterdam Weekly*, and watch for flyers and posters in record stores and around the city, to try to tap into some of this musical energy.

VENUES

Bourbon Street

Leidsekruisstraat 6–8; tel: 020

Muziekgebouw

Piet Heinkade 1; tel: 020 788 2010; www.muziekgebouw.nl; box office (by phone): Mon–Fri noon–5pm; Tram: 16, 26; map p.131 E3

This modern music venue by the waterfront could go into any of the musical categories here, as although there are a great number of classical concerts you're just as likely to find world music and jazz artists playing. There are concerts most days, and often several at the weekends in different parts of the building, which is worth seeing in its own right, especially at night

when its contemporary stylishness shines across the water.

Muziektheater

Amstel 3; tel: 020 625 5455; www.muziektheater.nl; box office: Mon–Sat 10am–6pm, Sun 11.30am–2.30pm (on concert days box office stays open until the curtain goes up); Tram: 9, 14; map p.137 C4

The Muziektheater is also known as the Stopera *(see box, right)*, and is the home of the Netherlands Opera. It is a hugely impressive development that incorporates the town hall as well as the base for the Dutch National Ballet too. Many Amsterdammers have season tickets and prices are kept quite low, so you may have to try to book months ahead if you know the dates of your visit to Amsterdam.

Contemporary Music

Modern music thrives in Amsterdam. It's one of the main European concert stops for international artists who are touring – they all like to play Amsterdam, for various reasons. There are plenty of long-established mid-sized

The **Muziektheater** is also known as the Stopera, officially because it's home to both the town hall *(stadhuis* in Dutch) and the Netherlands Opera. Unofficially the name came from a campaign to stop the building of the complex, which required some City Centre housing to be torn down, to make way for what many people felt was an over-expensive home for the city's governors and the opera-loving elite. The building went ahead, and the result is a fine arts venue and a striking piece of architecture.

623 3440; www.bourbonstreet.nl; daily from 10pm; Tram: 1, 2, 5; map p.133 E2

Despite the New Orleans name, more often associated with jazz, a broad range of styles get an airing here, including modern jazz, soul, rock and traditional blues. There are concerts every night, and jam sessions too, and its location close to the Leidseplein means it's often packed and concerts can really take off.

Melkweg
Lijnbaansgracht 234a; tel: 020 531 8181; www.melkweg.nl; box office: daily from 4.30pm, hours vary depending on concerts and other shows; Tram: 1, 2, 5, 10; map p.133 D2

There are two concert theatres inside the Melkweg, a former dairy and a long-standing venue not only for music concerts but also cinema, photography, drama and other media events. For music, though, there is always a choice of concerts almost every night of the year, and it's a really eclectic place that has become an Amsterdam institution.

Paradiso
Weteringschans 6–8; tel: 020 626 4521; www.paradiso.nl; daily, hours vary with shows; Tram: 1, 2, 5; map p.133 D3

Cajun dance music, Chip Taylor and the Mighty Sparrow were all to be heard at the Paradiso within the space of a couple of weeks recently, and it shows the wide range of styles that play here. It's one of the city's best venues, for fans and artists alike, for the space, the acoustics and just the general good-time vibe of the place. It has two main concert theatres, but even the big hall is still an intimate place where the acts can get a great rapport going with the audience. Sometimes really big names like The Rolling

Right: there is a wide choice on offer at Concerto.

Stones might slip in a concert, so you have to check what's on here when you're in town.

Sugar Factory
Lijnbaansgracht 238; tel: 020 626 5006; www.sugarfactory.nl; box office: daily from 6.30pm; Tram: 1, 2, 5; map p.133 D2

From Turkish techno music to late-night jazz and pretty well any other style of music you can think of – and some you probably didn't even know existed – the Sugar Factory, right next to the acclaimed Melkweg, can provide it. There aren't shows every night, so check the programme, but at weekends it's open until dawn.

Jazz

Like Paris, Amsterdam has always been a magnet for musical immigrants, especially jazz musicians, who like its laid-back attitude to life. As a result a healthy jazz scene has developed, with numerous cafés, clubs and bars providing outlets for the local talent, and plenty of big-name visitors too.

VENUES
Bimhuis
Piet Heinkade 3; tel: 020 788 2188; www.bimhuis.nl; box office: Mon–Sat noon–7pm, 6.30–11pm on concert evenings; Tram: 16, 26; map p.131 E3

The Bimhuis was always regarded as the best jazz venue in Amsterdam, which is one reason it was chosen to transfer to the **Muziekgebouw** (see p.91) when it was built. It survived the move well, and lost none of its audience or atmosphere. It brings in star names from

Left: the music gets people dancing at Sugar Factory (top) and Paradiso (below).

overseas, as well as showcasing the city's own fine jazz musicians, but with regular musical journeys into other areas like Chicago blues or Asian music nights.

Brix
Wolvenstraat 16; tel: 020 639 0351; www.cafebrix.nl; daily 5pm–1am, Fri–Sat until 3am; Tram: 1, 2, 5; map p.133 E1

Brix Food 'n' Drink is a bar and restaurant that serves only starters, most people coming for a drink and to enjoy the laid-back atmosphere. There's live jazz two nights a week, with different guests on Sundays and then on Monday the house band plays early, and from 10.30pm onwards they showcase new talents. It's not as well-known as some places, so feels like more of a personal discovery when you find it.

Jazz Café Alto
Korte Leidsedwarsstraat 115; tel: 020 626 3249; www.jazz-cafe-alto.nl; daily from 9pm; Tram: 1, 2, 5; map p.133 D2

This small jazz café-bar is one of the most popular in the city so is often packed out, especially as it's in the busy Leidseplein area and attracts a lot of casual visitors too. It's almost but not exclusively a jazz place, and you may find blues or a little

smooth soul music there too, but there have been live gigs on almost every night for the last 20 years.

Music Shops

Blue Note
Gravenstraat 12; tel: 020 428 1029; Tue–Sat 11am–6pm, Sun noon–5pm; Tram: 1, 2, 4; map p.136 A1

Blue Note is Amsterdam's best jazz music shop, just north of Dam Square. Named after the famous Blue Note label, it stocks anything and everything jazz, from the earliest 20th-century recordings to the latest of what's happening now.

Boudisque
Haringpakkerssteeg 10–18; tel: 020 623 2603; www.boudisque.nl; Sun–Mon noon–6pm, Tue–Sat 10am–6pm, Thur until 9pm; Metro: Centraal Station; map p.130 C3

Just off Damrak down from Centraal Station is one of the best record stores in Amsterdam. It stocks both vinyl and CD, mainly rock, pop and club music, but with a good selection of African and other world music.

Concerto
Utrechtsestraat 52–60; tel: 020 623 522; www.concerto.nl; Mon–Sat 10am–6pm, Thur until 9pm; Tram: 4; map p.134 A2

Concerto is one of the widest-ranging music stores in the city, spread across several buildings as the address suggests. It covers every kind of music from classical and opera to pop and rock, from 45s to albums, CDs and vinyl, new and second-hand.

Distortion Records
Westerstraat 244; tel: 020 627 0004; www.distortion.nl; Tue–Fri 11am–6pm, Thur until 9pm, Sat 10am–6pm; Tram: 10; map p.130 A3

Great little record store in the Jordaan which sells mostly vinyl, though it does have some CDs on the racks. From soundtracks, soul and '70s music it covers everything through to electro, hip-hop, drum 'n' bass and house music.

As well as the conventional music venues, including those listed here, check listings magazines and posters for concerts being held in some of Amsterdam's churches. These happen quite regularly, are sometimes free, and are a perfect way to enjoy good music while also getting a feel for the history and atmosphere of the venue. *See also Churches and Synagogues, p.38–9.*

Nightlife

To some travellers Amsterdam is canals and art museums, to others it's cannabis and the Red Light District, but to party animals it's one of the nightlife capitals of the world. Amsterdammers may not have that extrovert Latino nature, but they do like to enjoy themselves. Combine that with liberal laws, a late-night mentality, and a creative ability to come up with offbeat ideas and make them work – and you've got the makings of a great party city. There are also some very sophisticated places here, fun palaces, outrageous clubs and no shortage of other options open until dawn.

Casinos

Holland Casino Amsterdam

Max Euweplein 62; tel: 020 521 1111; daily 1.30pm–3am; Tram: 1, 2, 5; map p.133 D3

Take your passport with you as ID to this, one of the biggest casinos in Europe, and you must also be over-18, though the dress code isn't as strict in laid-back Amsterdam as in some other countries. Here, you will find almost 600 gaming machines, and about 60 table and poker games, including one of Sic Bo, a Chinese dice game, and nine blackjack tables. There's also an on-site restaurant, and it's very central, close to Leidseplein.

Clubs

Escape

Rembrandtplein 11; tel: 020 622

> There isn't a lot of straight cabaret, so to speak, in Amsterdam. The scene is dominated by the many brilliant gay and lesbian clubs and bars (see Gay and Lesbian, p.59), and there's very little else.

1111; www.escape.nl; Thur 11pm–4am, Fri–Sat 11pm–5am, Sun 11pm–4.30am; Tram: 4, 9, 14; map p.134 A2

One of the oldest, biggest (holds over 2,000 people) and still one of the best clubs in Amsterdam, despite constant new kids on the block. It's got several areas, different themed nights and new attractions like Escape deLux, a more intimate and exclusive space, if you can get in. In short, you cannot be one of the Amsterdam party people without trying Escape.

Jimmy Woo

Korte Leidsedwarsstraat 18; tel: 020 626 3150; www.jimmy woo.com; Wed–Sun 11pm–3am, Fri–Sat until 4am; Tram: 1, 2, 5; map p.133 D2

Jimmy Woo is an Amsterdam legend. Everyone's heard of Jimmy Woo. If you get nodded through the door into the plush Chinese-style interior that spreads over two floors then you know you've arrived. Plenty of people do get knocked back, so look stylish but have another plan ready just in case. As well as

the decadent lounge there's dancing to DJs on the downstairs dance floor, which is always packed.

Lux

Marnixstraat 403; tel: 020 422 1412; daily 8pm–3am, Fri–Sat until 4am; Tram: 1, 2, 5; map p.133 D2

Lux is where bar melts into club, with its DJs pumping out good music while old movies show on screens above the bars. It attracts young media people (designers, writers) and has an arty atmosphere, relaxed at first but as the night goes on it definitely turns into a clubby scene, and the only bad thing

Left and below: glamorous lounging at Jimmy Woo.

houses are now smart hotels or atmospheric museums, but the Odeon building, which opened in 1662 as a brewery, is now one of the smartest clubs in town. It's lush, it's plush and over three floors you'll find a café, bar, restaurant, brasserie, event spaces and a nightclub in a surprisingly large hall. There are different themed nights; check the programme, and if you're in one of those moods when you don't know what you want to do, get into Odeon, hang out and drift around.

Odessa

Veemkade 259; tel: 020 419 3010; www.de-odessa.nl; Wed–Thur 4pm–1am, Fri–Sat 4pm–3am; Tram: 26

This club/bar/restaurant on a Russian boat moored in the docks, and where the restaurant turns into a disco at weekend, was high-impact when it first opened in Amsterdam. Some of the novelty's worn off for local people, but for visitors it's still likely to be an impressive Amsterdam experience. The music from the DJs is nothing out of the ordinary, but the setting's terrific and the drinks are reasonably priced – a major plus point.

you can say about it is that if you leave it too late, you can't get in as it's too small for its own good.

The Mansion

Hobbemastraat 2; tel: 020 616 6664; www.the-mansion.nl; Wed–Sat 6pm–late, restaurant Sun 6pm–1am; Tram: 2, 5; map p.133 D3

By the Vondelpark, The Mansion is an upmarket club which also has several cocktail bars and two Chinese restaurants where they only stop seating at midnight. It really is a mansion, once

belonging to the Dutch royal family, and the owners have kept to that plush, almost over-the-top grandeur. You'll have to queue to get in, and sometimes push through the crowds standing round when a celeb is in the vicinity (lots of them do end up here), but like it or not, The Mansion is one of *the* Amsterdam night experiences.

Odeon

Singel 460; tel: 020 521 8555; www.odeonamsterdam.nl; Club: Thur 11pm–4am, Fri–Sat 11pm–5am, Bar: Wed 6pm–1am, Thur–Sun 6pm–4am; Tram: 1, 2, 5; map p.136 A4

Many 17th-century canal

Right: the crowds hit the dance floor at Odeon.

Left: party people at Odeon *(see p.95).*

comedy attitude. For many years, too, the main comedy troupe was the English-speaking Boom Chicago, which set a precedent. Despite that, if you're not sure about the performance, call ahead and check. Unless, of course, you're one of those people who does speak Dutch.

Boom Chicago
Leidseplein 12; tel: 020 423 0101; www.boomchicago.nl; box office: Sun–Thur 11am–8.30pm, Fri–Sat 11am–11pm; Tram: 1, 2, 5; map p.133 D2
Boom Chicago were the first and can still claim to be the best in Amsterdam, not least for the scale and smoothness of their operation. They have several shows a night, every night of the week, and even organise comedy canal cruises and comedy classes too. The shows are all in English and include sketch shows, stand-up, improv and open mike nights. It's also just a fun and friendly place to hang out, with a restaurant and a bar, and usually a genial crowd of people.

Panama
Oostelijke Handelskade 4; tel: 020 311 8686; www.panama.nl; Thur–Sun 9pm–late, sometimes additional nights, see website; Tram: 26
Overlooking the Ij out in the eastern docklands, this may be out of the centre but it's always been in with the right people, and stays in. Like many Amsterdam places it's hard to define – club, restaurant, bar, even partly a theatre – but its regulars don't care. There might be live jazz in the restaurant and loud funk in the club, or a touring comedy revue, visiting DJs, anything.

Suzie Wong
Korte Leidsedwarsstraat 45; tel: 020 626 6769; www.jimmywoo.com; daily 8pm–3am, Fri–Sat until 4am; Tram: 1, 2, 5; map p.133 D2
Suzie Wong has the same owners as the celebrated Jimmy Woo, and a similar East-meets-West feel to it, but this is more of a laid-back lounge than a full-on pump-it-up club. It's known for its cocktails, which do pack a punch, and some nights that attract a rowdy crowd when it might be time to move on, but when the mood is right, there's no better place to kick back than Suzie Wong.

Comedy Clubs
There's a small but impressive comedy scene in Amsterdam, and a fair amount of it is in English. Lots of Amsterdammers speak English fluently (they have to, they say, as no one learns Dutch), and with a healthy number of visitors seeking entertainment, and visiting comedians who perform in the English language, that all makes for a cosmopolitan

Right: out and about in the Red Light District.

Comedy Café

Max Euweplein 43-45; tel: 020 638 3971; www.comedycafe.nl; shows daily 9pm, plus some late-night shows; Tram: 1, 2, 5; map p.133 D3

There's a mix of local and overseas comedy here, and so a mix of languages, but some acts show dexterity in switching from one to the other, reacting to the audience. There are open shows and talent shows as well as stand-up nights, and some late-night cabaret-style events too. There's a bar and restaurant as well, and the theatre space is only small, nice and intimate. Check the programme, and you may just want to check the likely language too.

Late-Night Transport

Getting around late at night is less of a concern in Amsterdam because it's always been a late-night city, so there are plenty of people around, and the centre is also pretty small, which makes walking back after a late night out less of a hassle. Just don't fall in a canal (it does happen).

Trams, buses and the city's small metro system run until midnight, and then after that there are a number of all-night buses, which run about every half-hour through to 7am. There are also usually plenty of taxis around in the main nightlife areas, and the drivers are used to people wanting to go home at all hours, right through until public transport starts up again at about 6am. During the day taxis aren't the best choice for getting round Amsterdam, but at night when the streets are quieter they can zip around much more quickly.

The Red Light District

There is, you'll be astonished to hear, plenty of nightlife in Amsterdam's Red Light District. There are even some regular bars, clubs and late-night cafés there, but of course that's not why most people are visiting. The shows on offer range from live sex to raunchy to just plain teasing, and not all doorways are what they seem. Touts will offer you whatever it is they think you're looking for,

Seeing Amsterdam by night doesn't have to involve clubbing or the Red Light District. The aptly named Josephine Moons runs **Moonwalks**, on the night of the full moon each month. The programme varies, and covers Chinatown for the Chinese New Year, and areas like the Jewish Quarter, the Jordaan and the docklands at other times. Details at www.fullmoonwalk.nl.

and some of it can be pretty hardcore stuff. If you're at all uncertain, but still curious, you should head straight for one of the longer-estab-lished clubs that are now rip-off joints, such as the **Casa Rosso** (Oudezijds Achterburgwal 106–108), the **Moulin Rouge** (Oudezijds Achterburgwal 5–7) or the infa-mous **Bananenbar** (Oudezijds Achterburgwal 37), whose name gives you a hint of what to expect. Otherwise, contact one of the compa-nies offering organised tours of the Red Light District, with or without admission to an actual show, and satisfy your curiosity safely.

Palaces and Houses

With their decorative brickwork and ornate gables, Amsterdam's canalside houses have made the city iconic. They have provided inspiration for painters ever since the Dutch Golden Age and have accommodated not just wealthy merchants, but also religious orders, churches, synagogues, artists' studios and guilds. These listings offer the highlights, but see also *Museums and Galleries, p.78–89*, for collections housed in other fine buildings and *Architecture, p.28–9*, for more on the style of the city's buildings.

The Begijnhof

Access from Gedempte Begijnensloot or north side of Spui;
chapel tel: 020 622 1918;
www.begijnhofamsterdam.nl;
daily 9am–5pm; free; Tram: 1, 2,
5; map p.136 A3

The Begijnhof is a magnificent cobblestone courtyard of 17th-century buildings, hidden just a few steps away from some of the city's busiest shopping streets. It was founded in 1346 as a community for Catholic lay sisters – the beguines – who chose to lead a partial form of convent life, including

taking the vow of chastity. The last beguine died in 1971 (her house at No. 26 has been preserved as she left it), but the almshouses continue as a residential sanctuary, the quaint dwellings occupied by unmarried retired ladies 'of good repute'.

In the 15th century, this religious quarter was literally an island, and although the filling-in of the once-polluted Begijnensloot moats was made complete in 1865, the Begijnhof remains a place apart from the rest of the city.

On the southwest edge of the Begijnhof, at no. 34, is Amsterdam's oldest house, **The Wooden House** (Het

Houten Huis). Its facade dates from the 1470s, before building in wood was outlawed (in 1521) after a series of catastrophic fires.

Also in the south of the square stands the **English Reformed Church** (Engelse Kerk), built around 1400, while a Catholic church is contained within two houses (nos 29 and 30) that were secretly converted in 1665. The Begijnhof was the scene of the Miracle of Amsterdam, celebrated in the festival **Stille Omgang**. In 1345, a dying man was given the last rites and promptly vomited. His spew was thrown onto the fire, but the next day the communion wafer he had

The Amsterdam Stock Exchange, or Beurs *(see right)*, has been given the name of the man who designed it, Hendrik Petrus Berlage. Berlage was born in Amsterdam in 1856 and travelled throughout Europe, being influenced by the foreign architects that he met and the emerging styles that he saw. He also designed the bridge across the Amstel that bears his name, the Berlagebrug, and the impressive Gemeentemuseum in The Hague.

Left: the tower of the Beurs van Berlage.

Left: the Royal Palace *(see p.100)* dominates Dam Square.

lights. Guided tours of the building are organised by Artifex Travel (tel: 020 620 8112).

Canal Houses

Brouwersgracht, Herengracht and Singel; Tram: 1, 2, 5, 13, 17, bus 18, 21, 22; map p.136 B2–3

Around the eastern end of **Brouwersgracht** are some particularly fine merchants' houses. The canals themselves were built on the prosperity of the new Dutch Empire, and just to the north of Brouwersgracht is the old centre of that wealth, the **West Indies House** (West Indisch Huis) at nos 93–97 Herenmarkt. It was constructed in 1617, and then rented to the Dutch West India Company from 1623 as its headquarters. When the naval hero Admiral Piet Hein captured a Spanish silver fleet off Cuba in 1628, a prodigious booty of silver was stored here. It was also here that the decision to sell Manhattan Island for 60 guilders was made. In the courtyard you can see the statue of Peter Stuyvesant, the governor of New Amsterdam (as New York was then known).

Bearing south from Brouwersgracht is another canal, Herengracht. At no's 70–72 is the particularly elegant **House with the Pilaster Gable** (Het Huis met de Pilastergevel), dating from 1642. The next canal along (to the east) is Singel, where at no. 7 you can see the narrowest house front in Amsterdam, just 1m (3ft) wide. In the 17th century, taxes were levied on property owners according to the width of their house frontage – the maximum permissible

previously swallowed was found, untainted by fire or digestion, and the man miraculously recovered.

SEE ALSO CHURCHES AND SYNAGOGUES, P.38; FESTIVALS AND EVENTS, P.50

Beurs van Berlage

Damrak 243; tel: 020 620 8112 (for guided tours); www.beurs vanberlage.nl; opening hours vary with exhibitions; café Mon–Sat 10am–6pm, Sun 11am–6pm; Tram: 4, 9, 14, 16, 24, 25; map p.136 B1

Formerly the Amsterdam Stock Exchange, this remarkable building now functions as a cultural centre. It was constructed between 1896 and 1903 to designs by Hendrik Petrus Berlage, and for many years was considered the most important Dutch *fin*

Left: the distinctive gables of canal houses.

de siècle architectural monument. The architect Berlage *(see box, p.98)* used much cleaner and simpler lines than had been seen in the city before, and also used one of his favourite materials: brick. It was a startling change in a city used to elaborate and heavy neo-Gothic buildings, or tall and graceful canal houses. It is no longer used as the Stock Exchange, but is a conference and concert venue, though guided tours can be arranged and it has a pleasant café. As well as hosting exhibitions, it is now home to the Netherlands Philharmonic Orchestra, and there is a large concert hall (as well as a smaller one made of glass). The building's interior is an impressive mix of decorative brickwork, wooden flooring, stone pillars, narrow arcades, Romanesque and neo-Renaissance motifs, and steel roof girders from which hang pendular globe-shaped

stands today dates mainly from the 14th century. The interior, however, is a recreation of the castle as it was when the poet and historian P.C. Hooft resided here in the 17th century, when it was the meeting place of the illustrious Muiden Circle of poets and writers.

De Pinto Huis

Sint Antoniesbreestraat 69; tel: 020 616 7623; Mon–Wed 2–8pm, Fri 2–5pm, Sat 11am–4pm; free; Metro: Nieuwmarkt; map p.137 C3

Isaac de Pinto, a Portuguese Jew who fled to the Low Countries to escape the Inquisition's clutches, was one of Amsterdam's wealthiest merchants. He bought this building in 1651 and made substantial alterations over the next 30 years, adding elaborate painted panels and spectacular ceilings, as well as an ornate Italian Renaissance-style exterior. Having survived the threat of demolition and redevelopment in the 1970s, the house has since found a new function as a public library.

width was 10m (33ft), but the depth could extend to 60m (195ft). As a result, many houses were built narrow but deep, 'end-on' to the canals.

East Indies House (Oost Indisch Huis)

Kloveniersburgwal 48; tel: 020 525 2258; access to courtyard only; free; Tram: 4, 9, 14, 16, 24, 25; map p.136 C3

This imposing red-brick

On the west side of the Singel canal is another curious household, the 'cat boat', which provides board and lodging for 'orphaned' cats. A little way further south on the same canal, the first bridge is the Torensluis, which in the 17th century housed a prison in the stonework of the bridge itself. The unfortunate souls incarcerated here frequently found themselves up to their waists in foul water as the level of the canal changed with the incoming tides.

building dates from the 16th century and was rented by the **United East India Company** (Vereenigde Oostindische Compagnie) in 1603 for its headquarters. It frequently received deliveries of precious commodities, such as spices, coffee, ebony and mahogany. Today, it is occupied by the University of Amsterdam, but you can enter the courtyard for a snoop around.

Muiden Castle (Muiderslot)

Herengracht 1, Muiden; tel: 029 425 6262; Apr–Oct Mon–Fri 10am–5pm, Sat–Sun noon–6pm, Nov–Mar Sat–Sun noon–5pm; Trains: 101 and 157 from Amstel station; map p.130 C3

The red-brick, moated castle of Muiden was built in 1285 by Count Floris V of Holland, the founder of many Dutch towns. He was murdered here in 1296 by nobles who opposed his policy of urban development. The castle as it

Royal Palace (Koninklijk Paleis)

Dam Square; tel: 020 620 4060; www.koninklijkhuis.nl; due to reopen after extensive renovations in June 2009; admission charge; Tram: 1, 5, 9, 16, 24; map p.136 A2

This building's construction began in 1648, at the height of the Dutch Golden Age, under the aegis of architect Jacob van Campen. A total of 13,659 wooden piles – a figure all Dutch school children learn – were driven into the sandy soil to provide foundations. It was originally intended as a new town hall, and indeed, while under construction, the old medieval town hall it was replacing burnt down (a scene captured by Rembrandt).

The exterior's best aspect is its rear side, where an allegorical figure of Amsterdam struggles against the Ij and Amstel rivers. The sandstone dome above houses a carillon of bells from the 1660s by François Hemony, and is topped by a weathervane in the shape of a sailing ship.

In contrast with the exterior, the interior is light and elegant, decked out with white marble, carved reliefs, ornamentation and sculptures by the Flemish artists Artus Quellin the Elder and Rombout Verhulst. Among the state rooms are the **Citizens' Chamber** *(Burgerzaal)*, in which Amsterdam is represented as the centre of the world in a map carved on the floor; the **Council Chamber** *(Schepenzaal)*, with its paintings by Ferdinand Bol, Govert Flinck, Jan van Bronkhorst and Jacob de Wit; and the **Tribunal** *(Vierschaar)*, where court cases were heard.

The building was transformed from a town hall into a royal palace in 1808, when Louis Bonaparte, the short-reigning King of Holland (and brother of Napoleon Bonaparte), came to Amsterdam. He furnished it with Empire furniture, clocks and chandeliers. The palace became state property in 1936, though by Act of Parliament is put at the Queen's disposal for official state functions.

Right: there is a bustling market held today outside De Waag.

Above: De Pinto Huis.

De Waag

Nieuwmarkt 4; free; metro Nieuwmarkt; map p.137 C2

The bulky form of the Waag (or Weigh House) was originally built in 1488 as one of the city's fortified gateways – the Sint-Antoniespoort (St Anthony's Gate). It was here that Amsterdam's public executions took place. As the city expanded beyond the old walls, however, the gate became redundant, and so, around 1617, was rebuilt as a weigh house for checking the weight of ships' anchors and ordinance.

Later on, it changed function again, becoming a guild house for the civic guards, the stonemasons and also the surgeons. The octagonal tower at the centre was added around 1690 and housed the dissecting room where the Surgeons' Guild gave lessons in anatomy. The guild commissioned Rembrandt's famous painting *The Anatomy Lesson* of Dr Nicolaas Tulp (now in the Mauritshuis in The Hague).

Today, the building is home to the Waag Society (tel: 020 557 9898; www.waag.org), an organisation that promotes internet technology among different social sectors, and also a restaurant, In de Waag (tel: 020 422 7772; www.indewaag.nl).

About 5,000 Amsterdamers live on converted barges, floating concrete slabs and other water-borne vessels. This way of life is, however, highly regulated. The number of canalside moorings is fixed at 2,600, and, owing to the finite supply, they do not come cheap.

Parks and Gardens

With their passion for tulips, land reclamation and the associated water features, the Dutch are known for being keen on their parks and gardens. Such green spaces are also essential for the social wellbeing of one of the most densely populated, urbanised countries in the world. The city itself has about 30 public parks on its official list, ranging in size from little more than the size of a courtyard to over 900 hectares (2,200 acres). In addition, there are numerous private gardens, many of which are occasionally open to the public.

Amstelpark

Europaboulevard, Buitenveldert; tel: 020 644 4216; daily 24 hours; free; Tram: 4; Metro: RAI; Bus: 62

Situated in a suburb in the southwest of Amsterdam, this park was created in 1972 for the **Floriade**, a large flower and garden show that takes place every 10 years in the Netherlands. It features a valley with 8,000 rhododendron bushes in 139 varieties, a rose garden, a Belgian cloister garden, a butterfly garden, a nursery, a glass house and an orangery. There is also a well-preserved windmill dating back to 1636. For children, there is a playground (www.speeltuinamstelpark.nl), mini-golf, model farm, pony rides and a hedge maze. A miniature train runs through the park from April to October.

Amsterdamse Bos

Koenenkade 56; tel: 020 643 1414; www.amsterdamsebos.nl; daily 24 hours; free; Tram: 5; Bus: 170, 172

Occupying an area of some 900 hectares (2,200 acres),

In June, usually on the third weekend, some 20 of the grandest houses lining the city's canals open their private gardens to the public (tel: 020 320 3660; www.opengarden days.nl). The purchase of a ticket also entitles you to make use of the boat that ferries you to each of the venues.

this forested park is the largest in Amsterdam. It was created in the 1930s as part of a scheme to reduce unemployment, and you can learn all about its history in the visitors' centre (daily noon–5pm), near the main entrance. The park contains about 150 different tree species and a range of habitats for animal life, with marshland and reedbeds around Nieuwe Meer designated as nature reserves.

The **Cherry Blossom Park**, in the Japanese style, has over 400 flowering trees. There are also numerous water features in the park: a long rowing lake (the **Bosbaan**), several ornamental lakes and a number of swimming pools (including two shallow pools for children).

You can hire canoes, pedal boats and sailing dinghies. Permits for carp fishing can be obtained from the visitors' centre. Other sports include cycling (bicycles can be hired at the main entrance: tel: 020 644 5473), hockey, cricket and tennis. There are also two riding schools: **Manege Nieuw Amsterdam** (tel: 020 643 2468; www.nieuwamsterdam .nl) and **De Amsterdamse Manege** (tel: 020 643 1342; www.amsterdamse-manege.com). Then there is a large man-made hill (**De Heuvel**), with one slope left clear for winter sports. For children, there is an adventure playground, several farms (including one for goats) and a cheese factory (www.geitenboerderij.nl). In summer the Museumtram runs along the eastern side of the Bos (www.museum tram.nl). On evenings in July and August, plays are staged

Right: getting close to nature at the Hortus Botanicus *(see p.104).*

Left: relaxing with a picnic in the Sarphatipark *(see p.104)*.

and there is a swimming pool – and a shallower children's pool too.

Frankendael

Middenweg 72; tel: 020 423 3930; www.park-frankendael.nl; daily 24 hours; free; Tram: 9; Bus: 41; map p.135 E4

During the 17th and 18th centuries, many of Amsterdam's wealthiest citizens built summer retreats on reclaimed land to the east known as Watergraafsmeer. Frankendael is the last of these great estates to survive. The old house, with its elegant facade, was built in 1659 and, at the time of writing, is about to be reopened after renovation as a cultural and business complex. Visitors will be able to attend art exhibitions, lectures and even a small theatre. Behind the house is the so-called Style Garden, recreated as it was in the 1730s. Elsewhere, there is a fine botanical garden with over 500 varieties of plants and trees, many of them historic and rare. There are also areas landscaped in a more romantic style, with picturesque vistas among the mature trees.

at the open-air theatre (ww.bostheater.nl). The park even has its own campsite (tel: 020 641 6868).

SEE ALSO SPORTS, P.121

Beatrixpark

Diepenbrokstraat; tel: 020 546 450; www.vriendenbeatrix park.nl; daily 24 hours; free; Tram: 5

This pretty neighbourhood park is located behind the **RAI conference centre** in the south of the city. It was originally created between 1936 and 1938 and is now named after the Dutch queen. The park is in the informal English style, with a small lake, trees and lawns.

Flevopark

Insulindeweg 1002; tel: 020 692 5030; www.flevopark.nl; daily 10am–5.30pm; admission charge; Tram: 14

This large park was drained early last century, creating a large lake and several canals. Part of the 15.5-hectare (38-acre) site feels more like a nature reserve, with its reedbeds and plentiful birdlife (herons, swans, warblers and buntings). If sport is more your thing, though, the park is a popular place for jogging,

Gaasperplas Park

Amsteldijk Noord 55; tel: 020 496 5656; daily 24 hours; free; Bus: 59, 60, 174; Metro: Gaasperplas

Situated in the southeast of the city, this 160-hectare (395-acre) park was originally created in 1982 for the Floriade garden show. Today, the park is dominated by its large lake and water-sports centre. Activities on offer include swimming, rowing, canoeing, sailing and windsurfing. The rest of the park – with its rose gardens, azalea displays and decorative shrubbery – can be explored by bicycle or on horseback. The Gaasperping campsite is at the park's edge.

Hortus Botanicus

Plantage Middenlaan 2; tel: 020 625 9021; www.dehortus.nl; Mon–Fri 9am–5pm, Sat–Sun 10am–5pm, July–Aug until 7pm, Dec–Jan until 4pm; admission charge; Tram: 9, 14; Metro: Waterlooplein; map p.137 E4

The Hortus Botanicus was founded in 1638 for the cultivation of medicinal herbs for apothecaries. It moved to its current location in 1682 and now contains more than 4,000 different species of trees, shrubs and flowers in its gardens and seven greenhouses. It owes much of this diversity to the Dutch East India Company, which shipped in many species from the former colonies of Indonesia, Surinam and the Antilles in the 17th and 18th centuries. Highlights of the collection include the 300-year-old Eastern Cape giant cycad – the world's oldest recorded palm tree (in the Palm House). Look out also for the **Tri-Climate House**, a vast greenhouse with a subtropical section, a desert section and a tropical section. The 19th-century **Orangery**, meanwhile, has been converted into a pleasant café.

Keukenhof

Stationsweg 166a, Lisse; tel: 0252 465 555; www.keukenhof .com; mid-Mar–late May 8am–7.30pm; admission charge; Connexxion bus from Amsterdam centre – tickets sold at VVV tourist information offices

Spectacular park situated 30km (19 miles) southwest of Amsterdam. See literally millions of tulips in flower around lakes, pavilions, sculpture gardens and windmills.

Oosterpark

Oost-Watergraafsmeer; tel: 020 6080 608; daily 24 hours; free; Tram: 3, 7, 9; Bus: 22; map p.135 C3

This spacious park was established at the end of 19th century in the culturally diverse east of the city, just behind the **Tropical Museum** (Tropenmuseum). The park is most famous for its numerous sculptures, which include a monument commemorating the abolition of slavery in the Netherlands in 1861 and a memorial – entitled *The Scream* – to the film director Theo van Gogh, who was murdered in 2004 in a nearby street. Otherwise, the park is notable for its lake and birdlife – including grey herons and all kinds of ducks and geese. For children, there is a sectioned-off playground area.

SEE ALSO FILM, P.52; MUSEUMS AND GALLERIES, P.88

Sarphatipark

Ceintuurbaan; tel: 020 678 1678; daily 24 hours; free; Tram: 3, 4, 25; map p.134 A4

Situated in the fashionable De Pijp district, this recently renovated park was originally planned in the 1870s. At its heart is the grand monument to the doctor and philan-

Right: taking advantage of the sun at the Sarphatipark.

As well as numerous parks and gardens, Amsterdam has four beaches within easy reach of the City Centre: **NEMO Beach** (Oosterdok 2– created atop NEMO in the summer, *see Museums and Galleries, p.89*), **Citybeach** (Silodam), **Blijburg** and **Amsterdam Noord**.

Left: around the Oosterpark.
Right: pausing for a cycling
break in the Vondelpark.

thropist Samuel Sarphati
(1813–66), after whom the
park is named. Other features
include a picturesque lake,
three ornamental bridges, a
children's play area and
numerous cafés on the edge
of the park.

Vondelpark

Stadhouderskade; tel: 020
252 1252, theatre/concerts
info tel: 020 523 7790;
www.vondelpark.nl; daily 24
hours; free; Tram: 1, 2, 3, 5, 6;
map p.133 D3

Vondelpark's 45 hectares (120
acres) are visited by over 10
million people each year. It
was opened in 1865 and is
named after the German-born
poet and playwright Joost
van den Vondel (1587–1679),
who made Amsterdam his
home, and whose statue can
now be seen at the main
entrance. Originally, the park
was private and reserved for
the use of the wealthy families who lived nearby and
paid for its upkeep. Since
then, it has been embraced
by ordinary Amsterdamers as
a place for public events.
From June to August, the
park's open-air theatre

(www.openluchttheater.nl) hosts
concerts, theatre, comedy,
puppet shows and dance
performances on a daily, and
generally free, basis. Shows
specifically for children are
staged on Wednesday afternoons. In winter, if the ponds
freeze over, there are ice-
skating to be had. The rest of
the year, visitors have to
make do with rollerblading
(see also the mass event on
Friday evenings: www.friday
nightskate.com). Skates are
available for rent at **Snoep-
huisje** (near Amstelveenseweg entrance). For children,
there are seven play areas, as
well as numerous child-
friendly cafés. Between the
park entrances on Roemer
Visscherstraat and Vondelstraat, there is the **Filmmuseum** (www.filmmuseum.nl)
with a five-screen cinema.
There are screenings for
children on Wednesday and

Sunday afternoons.
SEE ALSO FILM, P.53

Westerpark

Haarlemmerweg 8–10; tel: 020
5810 400; www.westerpark.
amsterdam.nl; daily 24 hours;
free; Tram: 19; Bus: 21;
map p.130 A2

The original Westerpark was a
small green area established in
the 1890s next to a gasworks.
A century later, the long since
redundant gas-works were
converted into a cultural centre and the polluted wasteland
around it cleaned up and culti-
vated to make a much larger
park. The cultural centre
(www.westergasfabriek.nl)
includes a theatre, cinema,
artists' studios, gallery space,
a bakery and café. The park
itself has a children's pool and
play area and is a popular
place for a picnic. In the summer, the park hosts occasional
rock concerts.

Restaurants

W hen people say they know why you're going to Amsterdam, you can be sure that they're not talking about the cuisine. Amsterdammers don't like to take risks when they go out for a meal, preferring good company to gourmet delights – and on a sunny afternoon next to a lively canal, food does take second place. However, globetrotting local chefs are returning to the city and the standards of quality and imagination have risen quite sharply over the last few years, while there are also some fantastic Thai, Indonesian and Chinese restaurants. See also *Bars and Cafés, p.30–35* and *Food and Drink, p.54–7*.

City Centre

DUTCH
d'Vijff Vlieghen Restaurant
Spuistraat 294–302; tel: 020 530 4060; daily 5.30–10.30pm; Tram: 1, 2, 5; €€; map p.136 A3
Old-school Dutch cuisine doesn't get better treatment than at this elegant old restaurant. While locals come for the food, many tourists seem to pay more attention to their digital camera's display, especially in the beautiful Rembrandt Room.

INTERNATIONAL
Brasserie Harkema
Nes 67; tel: 020 428 2222; daily noon–4pm, 5.30–11pm; Tram: 4, 9, 14, 24, 25; €; map p.136 B3
One of the city's more modish eatery, this huge ex-tobacco factory serves up a short but sweet lunch menu and a dinner menu filled with brasserie

classics such as Caesar salad and simple steaks.

Luden
Spuistraat 304–306; tel: 020 330 5670; daily noon–midnight; Tram: 1, 2, 5; €; map p.136 A3
If you're searching for more than the usual café fare, Luden has an extensive lunch menu of brasserie classics in a great location overlooking the Singel that consistently attracts locals. Great wine list.

SPANISH
Joselito
Niuwendijk 2; tel: 020 622 7678; daily 11am–11pm; Tram: 1, 2, 5, 13, 17; €; map p.130 C3
When you're tired of the daytime sandwiches that most restaurants offer up, some Spanish tapas in the sun is a great idea. Joselito might be modest, but it's the decent portions of authentic tapas that make it so appealing.

Nieuwmarkt and the Red Light District

ASIAN
Nam Kee
Zeedijk 111–113; tel: 020 624 3470; daily noon–11pm; Tram: 4, 9, 16, 24, 25; €; map p.137 C2

Ignore the cheap décor, as this excellent Chinese restaurant has a loyal following who come solely for the food, especially the tasty roast duck and pork dishes. The memorable steamed oysters are so legendary they've inspired a book and a movie.
New King
Zeedijk 115–117; tel: 020 625 2180; daily 11.30am–midnight; Tram: 4, 9, 16, 24, 25; €; map p.137 C2
Great pan-province Chinese cuisine served in a more ele-

Right: immaculate food and surroundings at Vermeer.

Prices for an average two-course meal for one with a glass of house wine:
€€€   over €60
€€   €30–60
€   under €30

Left and Below Left: the stylish Brasserie Harkema.

Many Amsterdam hotels and guesthouses make a separate charge for breakfast, and it's a good idea to sample what's on offer before committing yourself to taking it for your whole visit. Some offer generous buffets, fresh juice and good coffee, but others can be minimal Continental breakfasts, hardly worth having. Cafés everywhere open early for business, and you might find yourself a better alternative there.

gant interior than most Asian restaurants in the area. The excellent dim sum and expertly cooked duck are the stars of the show.

FRENCH
Vermeer
NH Barbizon Palace Hotel, Prins Hendrikkade 59; tel: 020 556 4885; Mon–Sat noon–2.30pm, 6–10pm; Tram: 26; €€€; map p.137 C1
A classic old-school Michelin-starred restaurant (with all that this entails), Vermeer goes out to impress with the big-name ingredients, such as lobster, as well as doing some fantastic

old French dishes such as sweetbreads. Dress for the occasion.

INTERNATIONAL
Supperclub
Jonge Roelensteeg 21; tel: 020 638 0513; Wed–Sat 8pm–1am; Tram: 1, 2, 5; €€€; map p.136 A2
Supperclub is an Amsterdam original, where the food takes second place to the atmosphere of the all-white room. With your shoes off and your food balanced in your lap as you lounge around on a bed, this can be taken as great fun – or several hours of interminable frustration.

ITALIAN
Vasso
Rozenboomsteeg 10–14; tel: 020 626 0158; daily 5–10pm; Tram: 4, 9, 14, 16, 24, 25; €€; map p.136 A3
Vasso is a gem of an Italian eatery with excellent antipasti and authentic pastas (they do a great tagliatelli with Bolognese sauce), in a restaurant that is stylish in a charming faux rustic Italian way.

Western Canal Belt and the Jordaan

DUTCH
Moeder's Pot Eethuisje
Vinkenstraat 119; tel: 020 623 7643; Mon–Sat 5.30–9.30pm; Tram: 3; €; map p.130 B2
'Mother's Pot' is like stepping

into an eccentric mother's kitchen. Cluttered and charming, the home-style cooking is filling and flavourful – the classic *stamppot* (mash with vegetables) has no peer in town.

ASIAN
NOA
Leidsegracht 84; tel: 020 626 0802; Mon–Sat 6pm–midnight, Sun from 1pm; Tram: 1, 2, 5; €€; map p.133 D2

Amsterdam has fallen in love with Asian cuisine, and NOA (Noodles of Amsterdam) is one of the most modish places to enjoy the city's latest obsession. The atmosphere and cocktails generally surpass the cooking, but it's all good fun.

Top Thai
Herenstraat 28; tel: 020 623 4633; daily 4.30–10.30pm; Tram: 1, 2, 5, 13, 17; €; map p.130 B4

While many of Amsterdam's Thai eateries go easy on the chillies, Top Thai satisfies aficionados who find need to mop their brow halfway though one of their excellent spicy salads. The starters are good to share – just make sure you're all in agreement on 'heat' levels!

FRENCH
Balthazar's Keuken
Elandsgracht 108; tel: 020 420 2114; Wed–Fri 6–11pm; Tram: 7, 10; €; map p.133 D1

An excellent French-Med restaurant set in a former blacksmith's workshop, it's now more of a culinary workshop, with a weekly three-course menu that is always fascinating, featuring the freshest ingredients prepared in the open kitchen. Outdoor tables during summer.

Chez Georges
Herenstraat 3; tel: 020 626 3332; Mon–Tue, Thur–Sat 6–10pm; Tram: 1, 2, 5, 13, 17; €€; map p.130 B3

Intimate and inviting, this tiny restaurant is a love letter to all things Burgundian. Chef-patron Georges Roorda really knows how to indulge his guests, so take the full menu and relax. You're in safe hands.

Christophe
Leliegracht 46; tel: 020 625 0807; Tue–Sat 6.30–10.30pm; Tram: 13, 14, 17; €€€; map p.130 B4

While Christophe himself has moved on and the restaurant has had a makeover, you'd wonder what is left of the restaurant that held its Michelin star for so long. However, the change appears to have breathed new life into one of the city's finest restaurants. Modern inventive French cuisine at it's best, with an excellent wine list.

Jean Jean
Eerste Anjeliersdwarsstraat 14; tel: 020 627 7153; Tue–Sun 6–10pm; Tram: 3, 10; €–€€; map p.130 B3

This is a friendly, stylish, local restaurant, serving up fine and refined French favourites. Tables are quite close together, giving it a romantic, modern French bistro feel.

Prego
Herenstraat 25; tel: 020 638 0148; daily 6–10pm; Tram: 1, 2, 5, 13, 17; €€; map p.130 B3

A great split-level restaurant that serves some very interesting and expertly cooked, seasonal French cuisine. Expect dishes such as *coq au vin*, lamb and fillet of beef served with a twist.

De Struisvogel
Keizersgracht 312; tel: 020 423 3817; daily 6–11pm; Tram: 13, 14, 17; €; map p.133 D1

A favourite in the area, this charming basement restaurant goes with whatever ingredients are fresh, including ostrich steaks. ('The ostrich' is the name of the restaurant.) The short blackboard menu is your guide and the food is also great value.

Zuid Zeeland
Herengracht 413; tel: 020 624 3154; Mon–Fri noon–2.30pm, daily 6–11pm; Tram: 1, 2, 5; €€; map p.133 E2

This serious, but friendly, eatery has been consistently turning out great plates of

Left: luxury style at Christophe.
Right: the romantic Chez Georges.

Right: French cuisine in cheerful surroundings at Zuid Zeeland.

French favourites for years – and has a decent lunch menu as well.

INTERNATIONAL
De Belhamel
Brouwersgracht 60; tel: 020 622 1095; Sun–Thur 6–10pm, Fri–Sat 6–10.30pm; Tram: 1, 2, 5, 13, 17; €€; map p.130 B3
Even if the food wasn't as good as it is people would still come here to soak up the Art Nouveau ambience of the gorgeous interior. Thankfully the menu, which features French, Italian and Dutch cuisine, manages to be both original and exciting, and the great views from the outside tables make it hard to decide where to sit in summer.

Bordewijk
Noordermarkt 7; tel: 020 624 3899; Tue–Sun 6.30–10.30pm; Tram: 3; €€€; map p.130 B3
Contemporary and creative, Bordewijk's cuisine is some of the best in Amsterdam. Expect French-inspired food relying on classic French staples such as truffles and duck, but with a knowing nod to Asia and Italy. A great wine list and popular summer outdoor terrace (book ahead).

Damsteeg
Reestraat 28–32; tel: 020 627 8794; daily 6–10.30pm; Tram: 13, 14, 17; €€; map p.133 D1
Right near the Anne Frank House, Damsteeg is a smart space in a classic Amsterdam canalside house. A seafood-heavy menu sees modern updates of French, Dutch and global brasserie favourites, while the adjoining bar 'wine & bites' is excellent for snacks and wines by the glass.

Envy
Prinsengracht 381; tel: 020 344 64 07; Mon–Thur 6pm–1am, Fri–Sat noon–3pm, 6pm–3am, Sun noon–3pm, 6pm–1am (kitchen closes 11pm all days); Tram: 13, 14, 17; €; map p.133 D1
This modish restaurant may be achingly hip but it generally hits the mark with its excellent tasting menu. It can occasionally be inconsistent, however, and the service off-hand, but when it's good, it's fabulous.

Morlang
Keizersgracht 451; tel: 020 625 2681; daily 11am–1am; Tram: 1, 2, 5; €; map p.133 E2
If you can acquire a canalside table at this popular eatery,

it's worth settling in to sample a menu that takes a wild ride around the world's more popular cuisines while taking in the canal action.

Uyt
Runstraat 17d; tel: 020 627 0618; daily 6–11pm; Tram: 1, 2, 5; €; map p.133 D1
A great local favourite in the Nine Streets neighbourhood, the eclectic menu here is matched by an equally eclectic wine list, and the cooking is consistently good.

FUSION
Proeverij 274
Prinsengracht 274; tel: 020 421 1848; daily 6–10pm; Tram: 13, 14, 17; €; map p.133 D1
A fascinating restaurant that rewards diners who have a sense of adventure, Proeverij experiments wildly but to great success, with a mix of French and International

---

The Dutch tend to eat early in the evenings. Some restaurants open as early as 5pm, and many may be closed by 10pm, so watch out for this if you're a night owl. You will find places open later, but you'll have to look harder for them.

Left and Below Right: the canalside Le Zinc...et Les Autres offers delicious food that matches the charming setting.

a homely old canal house, has a menu that matches the ambience and a wine list to linger over.

ITALIAN
Pastini
Leidsegracht 29; tel: 020 622 1701; daily 6–10pm; Tram: 1, 2, 5; €; map p.133 D2
This lovely Italian canalside restaurant doesn't just rely on its picturesque location to draw in diners. From the mercifully uncomplicated menu, start with the antipasto misto followed by whatever delicious fresh pasta takes your fancy. Desserts are divine, and the wine list is a short trip through Italy. Book ahead.

cuisines. Grab an outside table on the cobblestones on a summer's evening and watch the world go by.

ITALIAN
Toscanini
Lindengracht 75; tel: 020 623 2813; daily 6–10.30pm; Tram: 3; €€; map p.130 B3
This classic Italian restaur-

The streets around Leidseplein are packed full of places to eat. There is a dizzying choice of cuisines on offer, from the ubiquitous steakhouses to cosy Indonesian eateries offering *rijsttafel (see Food and Drink, p.55)*, Italian pizza joints, Greek cantinas and even a few places serving traditional Dutch food. The quality is known to vary widely, but if you are undecided about what food you fancy, or just want a well-priced meal, these are fertile hunting grounds.

ant serves authentic pan-Italian favourites (including fresh pastas and risotto cooked to order) and has a comprehensive Italian wine list to boot. Book ahead.

Southern Canal Belt and Leidseplein

AFRICAN
Pygma-Lion
Nieuwe Spiegelstraat 5; tel: 020 420 7022; Tue–Sat 11am–10pm; Tram: 16, 24, 25; €€; map p.133 E2
While the thought of eating Bambi (antelope carpaccio) might be too much for some to bear, this modish South African restaurant is one of the city's best.

FRENCH
Le Zinc...et Les Autres
Prinsengracht 999; tel: 020 622 9044; Tue–Sat 5.30–11pm; Tram: 16, 24, 25; €; map p.134 A3
This delightfully romantic French restaurant, located in

Eastern Canal Belt and Rembrandtplein

DUTCH
Piet de Leeuw
Noorderstraat 11; tel: 020 623 7181; Mon–Fri noon–11pm, Sat–Sun 5–11pm; Tram: 16, 24, 25; €; map p.133 E3
This meat-lovers' favourite specialises in all kinds of beef – but the liver with bacon and herring on toast are notable.

ASIAN
Take Thai
Utrechtsestraat 87; tel: 020 622 0577; daily 6–11pm; Tram: 4; €; map p.134 A2
While this contemporary all-white Thai restaurant looks like it would be too stylish to be authentic, the kitchen delivers real chilli-hot Thai cuisine. Try the fantastic starter plate and fine curries.
Tempo Doeloe
Utrechtsestraat 75; tel: 020 625 6718; daily 6–11.30pm; Tram: 4; €€; map p.134 A2

This landmark Indonesian restaurant has managed to maintain their standards over the years as newcomers try to surpass it in the rice and rendang stakes. Don't skip the desserts.

Zushi
Amstel 20; tel: 020 330 6882; daily noon–11pm; Tram: 4, 9, 14; €; map p.136 B4

Zushi serves up conveyor-belt Japanese sushi that is a cut above the competition due to the excellent soups and grills that surpass the fairly standard sushi.

FRENCH
Silex
Kerkstraat 377; tel: 020 620 59 59; Tue–Sat 6–10pm; Tram: 4; €€; map p.134 A2

Very creative Mediterranean-influenced French cuisine is

the calling card of this fine split-level restaurant that attracts a knowing local crowd. Excellent wine list.

ITALIAN
La Storia Della Vita
Weteringschans 171; tel: 020 623 4251; Mon–Sat 6–11pm; Tram: 6, 7, 10; €; map p.133 E3

Old-school Italian best encapsulates the atmosphere and menu of this authentic restaurant, so be sure to order up fine Italian classics such as gnocchi.

Segugio
Utrechtsestraat 96; tel: 020 330 1503; 6–11pm Mon–Sat; tram 4; €€; map p.134 A3

Segugio serves up sophisticated Italian fare in a romantic atmosphere with plenty of premium ingredients, such as scallops, to make the night something special.

The Museum Quarter, Vondelpark and the South
ASIAN
Blue Pepper
Nassaukade 366; tel: 020 489 7039; dinner; Tram: 1, 6; €; map p.133 D2

Blue Pepper's take on contemporary Indonesian cuisine is a revelation. Fine wines and excellent, multi-course menus, packed with flavour and invention, ensure the night goes smoothly.

De Pijp is the place to go if you're after cheap and authentic ethnic choices: the area around the Albert Cuypmarkt is a particularly good place to look. For something different, consider Surinamese food (see Food and Drink, p.56).

Khorat Top Thai
2e C. Huygenstraat 64; tel: 020 683 1297; daily 4–10pm; Tram: 3, 12; €; map p.133 C3
This modest Thai eatery serves up lashings of great Thai classics such as Tom Kha Gai (chicken soup with coconut milk). It's close to the Vondelpark as well – making for a wonderful picnic if you want takeaway.

FRENCH
Le Garage
Ruysdaelstraat 54; tel: 020 679 7176; Mon–Fri noon–2pm, 6–11pm; Tram: 16; €€€; map p.133 D4
It may be frequented by local celebrities, but don't let this deter you from the imaginative French haute cuisine dishes coming out of the kitchen. If the pretension does put you

off, there is a more casual version of the eatery next door.

Jodenbuurt, the Plantage and the Oost
FRENCH
La Rive
Professor Tulpplein 1; tel: 020 622 6060; Tue–Fri noon–2pm, Tue–Sat 6.30–10.30pm; Tram: 6, 7, 10; €€€; map p.134 B3
Romantic La Rive might have lost a Michelin star, but it has lost none of its appeal, with lovely views of the Amstel, polished French cuisine and a hefty wine list.

The Waterfront
SEAFOOD
Eenvistweevis
Schippersgracht 6; tel: 020 623 2894; Tue–Sun 6–10pm; Tram: 9, 14; €; map p.134 C1
Far away from the crowds, this beloved local Schippersgracht eatery serves up simple fresh seafood cooked chosen from a handwritten daily menu.

De Pijp
ASIAN
Yamazato
Hotel Okura Amsterdam,

Ferdinand Bolstraat 333; tel: 020 678 7111; daily 7.30–9.30am, noon–2pm, 6–9.30pm; Tram: 12, 25; €€€
As everyone knows, great Japanese cuisine is never inexpensive, and this Michelin-starred restaurant is certainly proof of that – but the amazingly fresh sushi on offer is worth every euro.

EUROPEAN
Trèz
Saenredamstraat 39–41; tel: 020 676 2495; Tue–Thur, Sun 6–10pm, Fri–Sat 6–11pm; Tram: 16, 24, 25; €€; map p.133 E4
The tables at this popular restaurant are almost always as packed as their fantastic Trèz 'tapas' platter, which everyone shares as a starter. The menu, which is Mediterranean mixed with Dutch influences has hearty main courses as well. Book ahead.
Zaza's
Daniël Stalpertstraat 103; tel: 020 673 6333; Mon–Wed 6–10.30pm, Thur–Sat 6–11pm; Tram: 16, 24, 25; €; map p.133 E4

This petite restaurant has a strong local following for its friendly service and fine cooking. The eclectic menu could feature anything from Beef Wellington to home-made ravioli.

FRENCH

Ciel Bleu

Hotel Okura Amsterdam, Ferdinand Bolstraat 333; tel: 020 678 7450; daily 6.30–10.30pm; Tram: 12, 25; €€€

This French restaurant earns its Michelin-starred status with sophisticated and seasonal French fare, attentive service and an extensive wine list. There are interesting set menus as well as à la carte.

Le Hollandais

Amsteldijk 41; tel: 020 679 1248; Mon–Sat 6.30–10.30pm; Tram: 3, 4; €€; map p.134 B4

The flavours of French regional cooking simply waft out the entrance of this split-level restaurant that specialises in free-range meats (including game) and shellfish. Notable wine list and knowledgeable service.

FUSION

Puyck

Ceintuurbaan 147; tel: 020 676 7677; Mon–Sat 5.30–10.30pm; Tram: 3, 24, 25; €; map p.134 A4

In a section of Ceintuurbaan more noted for computer shops than fine cooking, Puyck's fusion cuisine combines mainly French and Asian influences to stunning effect.

INDIAN

Balti House

Albert Cuypstraat 41; tel: 020 470 8917; daily 4–11pm; Tram: 16, 24, 25; €; map p.133 E4

While many cuisines are represented well in Amsterdam, Indian isn't generally one of them, with the notable exception of Balti House. Good hot curries and cold Kingfisher beer taken on the terrace are a great combination.

INTERNATIONAL

De Witte Uyl

Frans Halsstraat 26; tel: 020 670 0458; Tue–Sat 6pm–1am; Tram: 16, 24, 25; €€; map p.133 E3

Amsterdammers love this restaurant, especially during summer, when tables line the footpath. A diverse menu and

Prices for an average two-course meal for one with a glass of house wine:

€€€ over €60
€€ €30–60
€ under €30

a dedication to organic and free-range meats keep the locals happy.

Restaurant Altmann

Amsteldijk 25; tel: 020 662 7777; Tue–Fri noon–2pm, daily 6pm–midnight; Tram: 3; €€; map p.134 B4

This elegant restaurant attracts a well-to-do crowd who come for the seasonal menu crafted by well-known chef Mohammed Mahraoui, whose Moroccan background sees a fascinating Middle Eastern influence in some of the dishes.

MIDDLE EASTERN

Bazar

Albert Cuypstraat 182; tel: 020 675 0544; daily Mon–Thur 11am–1pm, 5–11pm, Fri 11am–2pm, 5pm–midnight, Sat 9am–2pm, 4.30pm–midnight, Sun 9am–midnight; Tram: 16, 24, 25; €; map p.134 A4

A welcome respite from the chaotic Albert Cuypstraat markets, the kitsch Middle Eastern style and authentic menu make this a great shopping stop.

Mamouche

Quellijnstraat 104; tel: 020 673 6361; daily 6–11pm; Tram: 16, 24, 25; €€; map p.133 E4

With everything Maghreb being popular in Amsterdam, this modish restaurant is fancier than most you'll actually find in the Maghreb. Thankfully, the Moroccan dishes such as lamb tagine and vegetable couscous are rendered authentically.

Left: Middle Eastern design at Bazar.

113

Shopping

Amsterdam's shops are as varied and as quirky as the rest of the city. Being a compact sort of place, it only has a few large department stores, but what it lacks in big outlets it more than makes up for with smaller individual stores. These include shops which only sell one kind of item, such as water or condoms, and any number of stylish boutiques. Naturally there are also shops selling two of the city's more notorious commodities: sex and drugs. For futher specialised shops, see *Dutch Design, p.42–3, Food and Drink, p.56–7, Literature, p.75, Markets, p.76–7,* and *Music, p.93*.

The Shopping Map

As well as there being shops that are specialist, there are parts of the city that specialise in particular kinds of shopping. You'll find designer names clustered on and around **PC Hoofstraat** near the Vondelpark, and along the **Leidsestraat** too. Many of the funkier shops and markets are in the **Jordaan**, where the **Nine Streets** area has become a focus for shops with a difference. The very centre, along **Damrak** and around the **Dam Square**, is like the centre of many cities – tourist stores, mass chain stores, and day-to-day shopping. And there are no prizes for guessing what you can buy in the **Red Light District**.

Antiques

Jan Beekhuizen
Nieuwe Spiegelstraat 49; tel: 020 626 3912; www.jan beekhuizen.nl; Mon–Sat 10am–6pm; Tram: 4, 9, 16; map p.133 E2
This shop specialises in pewter from the 15th–19th centuries but also has furniture and other antiques, and has been doing business here since 1945.

Cigars

PGC Hajenius
Rokin 92–96; tel: 020 623 7494;

Right: classic Delftware.

www.hajenius.com; Mon noon–6pm, Tue–Sat 9.30am–6pm, Sun noon–5pm; Tram: 4, 9, 14; map p.136 A3
Pantaleon Gerhard Coenraad Hajenius came to Amsterdam in 1826 and opened his first cigar shop, which later moved to this location in 1915, close to the Tobacco Exchange. Since then Amsterdam has become better-known for another type of smoking experience, but this is where you'll find the best choice of cigars from all over the world, along with general smoking paraphernalia. Even if you don't plan to buy, you should call into the store to see the elaborate Art Deco interior, complete with chandeliers and Italian marble.

Delftware

Delft Shop
Spiegelgracht 13; tel: 020 421 8360; www.delftshop.com; Mon–Sat 9.30am–6pm, Sun

Left: Metz & co is a department store selling chic designer goods.

Left: futuristic displays at Shoebaloo *(see p.118).*

Metz & co

Leidsestraat 34–36; tel: 020 520 7020; www.metzenco.nl; Mon 11am–6pm, Tue–Sat 9.30am–6pm, Sun noon–5pm; Tram: 1, 2, 5; map p.133 E2

Hugo Boss, Burberry, John Galliano, Valentino – just some of the designer names that the smart department store Metz & co stocks, along with Gucci perfume, Knoll furniture, Lalique glass and many other stylish gifts and accessories. The top-floor **M** restaurant is also as chic as the rest of the store.

Vroom & Dreesmann

Kalverstraat 203; tel: 0900 235 8363; www.vroomen dreesmann.nl; Mon 11am–6.30pm, Tue–Sat 10am–6.30pm, Thur until 9pm, Sun noon–6pm; Tram: 4, 9, 14; map p.136 A4

V&D carries an impressive array of goods in its huge store at the southern end of the city centre. It's the usual kinds of items, such as clothing, cosmetics, jewellery, kitchenware and leisure goods like CDs and DVDs. It's worth visiting for the sheer size of the shop, though, and if there's something you haven't packed then there's a fair chance you'll find it here... if you can find it, that is.

11am–6pm; Tram: 4, 9, 16; map p.133 E3

You don't have to go to Delft to buy some Delftware or Royal Delft porcelain, as this store is the official Amsterdam outlet. It doesn't just sell the current lines, but antique items too, and other well-known names like Waterford crystal and Lalique glassware.

Department Stores

De Bijenkorf

Dam 1; tel: 020 621 8080; www.bijenkorf.nl; Mon 11am–7pm, Tue–Wed 9.30am–7pm, Thur–Fri 9.30am–9pm, Sat 9.30am–6pm, Sun noon–6pm; Tram: 1, 2, 4; map p.136 A2

This is Amsterdam's most famous department store, right on Dam Square, with stunning views over the store from its excellent café. The name of the store means 'beehive', and you'll find out why as you try to make your way round the labyrinth of departments. It has the typical traditional mix of household goods and sensible clothing that you find in department stores worldwide, but there are some surprises including designer names, with some fun and funky clothing on the top floor which the teens and 20-somethings head for.

In many shops, wrapping the item is something of an art form in itself. Even in some fairly ordinary shops, like food stores, you might find that the assistant takes longer to wrap the gift than it took you to choose it. If you are actually buying a present for someone else, ask if there's any kind of special gift-wrapping service available. The results are usually stylish and very impressive.

115

Left: inspecting the gems at Coster Diamonds.

Diamonds and Jewellery

Amsterdam Diamond Center

Rokin 1–5; tel: 020 624 5787; www.amsterdamdiamond center.nl; Mon–Sat 10am–6pm, Thur until 8.30pm, Sun 11am–6pm; Tram: 4, 9, 14; map p.136 B2

This is the most central and the largest outlet in Amsterdam for buying diamonds, whether as individual stones or as finished rings, earrings, other jewellery, watches and diamond-encrusted items. You may get better prices and learn more at one of the diamond factory outlets, but here the choice is far greater.

Coster Diamonds

Paulus Potterstraat 2–6; tel: 020 305 5555; www.coster diamonds.com; daily 9am–5pm; Tram: 2, 5, 6; map p.133 D3

This is one of the best-organised of the diamond

Left: Dutchies sells colourful but smart leather bags.

factories, being by the Rijksmuseum and so handily placed for entertaining large tour groups. It is also one of the oldest and most experienced firms, dating back to 1840, and its shop has a very good range of its products. You don't have to take a tour in order to buy, but it will definitely help you learn more about what you're buying.

MK Jewelry

Reestraat 9; tel: 020 427 0727; www.mk-jewelry.com; Tue–Sat 11am–6pm; Tram: 13, 14, 17; map p.133 D1

This whole shop is a work of art with its multicoloured Murano glass chandelier, bold modern art on the walls and colourful chairs, but the chairs are also comfy, there's a fireplace, a coffee table and magazines to browse, while the jewellery designs on display (chains, rings, pearls, earrings) include both simple traditional and eye-catching modern designs. The store also has an outlet at: PC Hooftstraat 102; tel: 020 470 5404; Tue–Sat 11am–6pm; map p.133 D3.

Drugs

Conscious Dreams Dreamlounge

Kerkstraat 119; tel: 020 626

6907; www.consciousdreams.nl; Apr–Oct: daily noon–10pm, Nov–Mar: Wed–Sat noon–10pm; Tram: 1, 2, 5; map p.133 E2

There are several branches of Conscious Dreams in the Netherlands, including another in Amsterdam at Warmoesstraat 12 and going by the name of Conscious Dreams Kokopelli. They sell things like cannabis seeds and magic mushrooms, that you would expect to find in Amsterdam, but they also sell a bewildering range of other goods such as vitamin supplements, herbal extracts, royal jelly, wormwood (make your own absinthe), 'grow your own peyote' kits and Horny Goat Weed pills.

Hemp Works

Nieuwendijk 13; tel: 020 421 1762; www.hempworks.nl; Sun–Wed 11am–7pm, Thur–Sat 11am–9pm; Tram: 1, 2, 5; map p.130 C3

Hemp Works has been in business since 1993 and, yes, they sell cannabis seeds and magic mushrooms, but also a quality range of clothes and other products made from hemp. In fact they could almost be listed under 'Fashion' as they range from surfwear and hoodies to eco-friendly sandals and sneakers.

Fashion

Betsy Palmer

Rokin 9–15; tel: 020 422 1040; www.betsypalmer.com; Mon noon–6.30pm, Tue–Fri 10.30am–6.30pm, Thur until 9pm, Sat 10am–6pm, Sun 1–6pm; Tram: 4, 9, 14; map p.136 B2

Right: beautiful vintage finds at Laura Dols.

Many shops in Amsterdam are closed on Monday mornings as well as on Sundays, so if you're planning a weekend break then get your shopping done on Saturday. If staying longer, then Thursday is the usual late-night opening night. These aren't hard and fast rules, but shopping hours generally aren't as long as you would find in other European capital cities, though they are changing slowly. *See also Essentials, p.46.*

Friendly assistants and designs with a difference in this shoe shop, where Betsy Palmer is the fun in-house label but which also carries other ranges. Here you'll find dress shoes, some outrageously high heels, warm boots and fun Dutch clog designs, though the range changes constantly, so expect anything. Also at: Van Woustraat 46; tel: 020 470 9795; Mon noon–6pm, Tue–Fri 10am–6pm, Sat 10am–5pm; map p.134 A4.

Cellarrich
Haarlemmerdijk 98; tel: 020 626 5526; www.cellarrich.nl; Mon 1–6pm, Wed–Fri 11am–6pm, Sat 11am–5pm; Tram: 1, 2, 4; map p.130 B2
From stylish clogs to eye-catching bags and purses, wallets, jewellery and other accessories, this shop also specialises in leatherwear and the work of young, local designers. Definitely worth a look.

Dutchies
Runstraat 27; tel: 020 626 3001; www.dutchiesdesign.nl; Tue–Sat 11am–6pm, last Sun of month 2–5pm; Tram: 1, 2, 5; map p.133 D1
Owner-designer Linda Creemers was once a lawyer who changed career to open this store selling her own and others' leather and suede bags. They're done in limited editions of up to 20 maximum, and you can find bags that are stylish but suitable for business use, and also fun creations in pinks, reds and other bright colours.

Episode
Berenstraat 1; tel: 020 626 4679; www.episode.eu; Sun–Mon 1–6pm, Tue–Wed 11am–6pm, Thur 11am–8pm, Fri 11am–7pm, Sat 10am–7pm; Tram: 13, 14, 17; map p.133 D1
This gem of a vintage second-hand clothing shop also has outlets in London, Paris and other European cities, as well as its original Amsterdam branch at Waterlooplein 1 (tel: 020 320 3000). Because it's second-hand you never know quite what you'll find, from 1950s all-American girl (and guy) looks and 1960s pop gear to the 1970s and 1980s which form the bulk of the stock. It's all been cleaned and it's organised just like a new fashion store, so don't expect a market-style free-for-all.

Laura Dols
Wolvenstraat 6–7; tel: 020 624 9066; www.lauradols.nl; Mon–Sat 11am–6pm, Thur until 9pm, Sun 1–6pm; Tram: 1, 2, 5; map p.133 E1
Spread across two stores and basements, Laura Dols has been in business here for

117

30 years. It's mainly vintage clothing going back to the 1940s, but it also stocks unusual lines like vintage tablecloths, bed linen, tea towels and other items. These can include beautiful handmade lace, and there are some bargains to be found. Little wonder you'll find props buyers from TV shows and movies browsing here for period pieces.

Shoebaloo
Koningsplein 7; tel: 020 626 7993; www.shoebaloo.nl; Mon noon–6pm, Tue–Sat 10am–6pm, Thur until 9pm, Sun–6pm; Tram: 2, 3, 5; map p.136 A4

Gucci, Dior, Prada, Alexander McQueen, Miu-Miu – this is where you'll find these names, and more, in a store that began life in the 1970s selling hippie boots in the Jordaan. It became a well-known name around Amsterdam both for its relaxed style and the quality of its shoes. Today there's a more futuristic look to its stores, with several of them around the city and an expansion into the top design names and accessories.

Spoiled
Wolvenstraat 19; tel: 020 626 3818; www.spoiled.nl; Sun–Mon 1–6pm, Tue–Sat 10am–6pm, Thur until 9pm; Tram: 1, 2, 5; map p.133 E1

Adidas, Levi's, Tommy Hilfiger, Nike and Nudie are some of the brand names you'll find in this hip store that stocks not just street fashion but also books, magazines, gadgets, toys for the boys, and there's a hairdresser and café to chill out in as well.

Van Ravenstein
Keizersgracht 359; tel: 020 639 0067; www.van-ravenstein.nl; Mon 1–6pm, Tue–Sat 11am–6pm; Tram: 13, 14, 17; map p.133 D1

Smart boutique which sells the designs of some of the leading Belgian designers such as Viktor & Rolf, Martin Margiela, Dirk van Saenne and Dries van Noten. There's also a small bargain basement for reduced designer labels, but it's only open on Saturdays.

Young Designers United
Keizersgracht 447; tel: 020 626 9191; www.ydu.nl; Mon 1–6pm,

Right: saucy goodies at Stout.

Tue–Sat 10am–6pm; Tram: 13, 14, 17; map p.133 E2

YDU is exactly what it says it is – an opportunity for young designers to have their own label and showcase their designs at affordable prices. You can feel this ethos in the shop, as the assistants are enthusiastic about the work they sell, and it's certainly an opportunity to spot something different. Naturally many of the names are from the Netherlands, but there are also designers from London, South Africa, Barcelona, Austria – anything that the owners think is good.

Flowers

Gerda's Flowers
Runstraat 16; tel: 020 624 2912; Mon–Fri 9am–6pm, Sat 9am–5pm; Tram: 1, 2, 5; map p.133 D1

You may or may not want to take tulips from Amsterdam back home (though if you do, this store will deliver anywhere in the world), but

you should at least take a look at this famous flower shop. They're known for their floral arrangements and window displays, so even if you only take a photo, be sure to take a look.

Photography

Rock Archive

Prinsengracht 110; tel: 020 423 0489; www.rockarchive.com; Wed–Fri 2–6pm, Sat noon–6pm; free; Tram: 13, 14, 17; map p.130 B4

The Rock Archive is the Amsterdam branch of a select chain of stores selling limited-edition rock music photography, from Aerosmith to the White Stripes. They have some striking images of rock legends like Eric Clapton, Bo Diddley and The Beatles, and more contemporary artists such as Duffy and Amy Winehouse, all available in a variety of sizes and ready for wall mounting.

Sex

Absolute Danny

Oudezijds Achterburgwal 78; tel: 020 421 0915; www.absolutedanny.com; Mon–Sat 11am–9pm, Sun noon–9pm; Tram: 4, 9, 16; map p.136 C2

Left: the stylish shop floor at Van Ravenstein.

It calls itself the ultimate erotic and fetish wear company, so if you want outfits from feather to leather, or in materials you probably never thought of, head for the Red Light District outlet of Absolute Danny. The store also sells magazines, DVDs, sex toys and everything else you'd expect to find in this part of Amsterdam.

Condomerie

Warmoesstraat 141; tel: 020 627 4174; www.condomerie.com; Mon–Sat 11am–6pm; Tram: 4, 9, 14; map p.136 B2

In a city famous for its specialist shops, there had to be one. The Condomerie has been in business since 1987 and has since become renowned around the world for its choice of speciality: condoms. It's worth seeing if only for its window displays, but inside it's part shop and part museum, where you can learn everything there possibly is to know about the condom, and choose from thousands of varieties for sale. And no, one size doesn't fit all – but they have measuring advice if you need it.

Mail and Female

Nieuwe Vijzelstraat 2; tel: 020 623 3916; www.mail female.com; Mon–Sat 11am–7pm; Tram: 7, 10, 16; map p.133 E3

From chocolate body paint and massage oils to vibrators, bondage wear, sexy lingerie and intimate jewellery, you'll find it all at this well-known store. It's been around in the Netherlands a long time as a mail-order specialist, hence the name, and this is its retail shop, not in the Red Light District but actually fairly close to the Rijksmuseum.

Stout

Berenstraat 9; tel: 020 620 1676; www.stoutinternational.com; Mon–Fri noon–7pm, Sat 11am–6pm, Sun 1–5pm; Tram: 13, 14, 17; map p.133 D1

Stout offers sex with sophistication. Here in the Jordaan you'll find not just the expected things, such as DVDs with titles like 'Toy with Me', but sexy lingerie from famous names including John Galliano and Dolce & Gabbana. There are sex toys too, like blindfolds and handcuffs – something for all tastes.

Don't assume you can just use plastic wherever you go in Amsterdam. The Dutch generally prefer paying cash for goods, even for quite high amounts, and some of the smaller stores don't have credit card facilities, so make sure you've got plenty of euros to hand, just in case.

Sports

When it comes to sport, many people associate the Dutch with football – especially the players' lurid orange strip – and then also perhaps cycling or darts, hockey or swimming. The Dutch are, of course, good at all these things, but there are also several other activities that you might not have expected to be so popular in the Netherlands. Baseball and American football have quite a following, both in terms of spectating and participation. Then there is rock climbing – not the most obvious sport in a country as flat as a pancake – and, unusually for a non-Commonwealth country, cricket is also widely played.

American Football

The local professional team is the **Amsterdam Admirals** (www.admirals.nl), who, with cheerleaders in tow, get tough at the **Amsterdam ArenA** *(see Football, below)*. There is also an amateur team, the **Amsterdam Crusaders** (www.amsterdam-crusaders.nl). Both teams play under the aegis of the AFBN (www.afbn.nl), the sport's governing body in Holland.

Baseball

Baseball is known as *honkbal* in the Netherlands. The local side is the **Amsterdam Pirates** (www.amsterdam pirates.nl), who are among the best in Europe. They can be seen playing at the **Sportpark Ookmeer** in the west of the city (Herman Bonpad 1; tel: 020 613 4487) during the season – from April to October. See www.knbsb.nl for baseball competitions, fixtures and other information.

Climbing

Klimhal Amsterdam
Naritaweg 48; tel: 020 681 0121;

A popular game in the bars and cafes of Amsterdam and other Dutch cities is *carambole*, a variation on billiards where players score points by ricocheting off the cue ball and the opponent's ball.

www.klimhalamsterdam.nl; Mon, Tue, Thur 5–10.30pm; Wed 2–10.30pm; Fri 4–10.30pm; Sat 11am–10.30pm; Sun 9.30am–10.30pm; NS station: Sloterdijk
One of the country's largest climbing walls, with plenty to test the experienced climber. Lessons and courses available for beginners.

Cycling

The Dutch are a nation of cyclists, and the country is criss-crossed with cycle paths and routes. You can either hire a bike and set off independently, or take a group bike excursion (includes bike hire) – information from VVV *(see Essentials, p.49)*.
Sportpark Sloten
Sloterweg 1045; tel: 020 617 7510; Tram: 2
For cycling fanatics, this fea-

tures a 22km (12-mile) circuit and an indoor velodrome. Two cycle clubs are based here: **ASC Olympia** (www.ascolympia.nl) and **WV Amsterdam** (www.wv amsterdam.nl).
SEE ALSO ENVIRONMENT, P.45; TRANSPORT, P.125

Darts

Darts has a high profile in Holland, thanks to Raymond 'Barney' Barneveld, the winner of numerous world titles. If you want to see the big man play, consult the tournament calendar at www.ndb darts.nl. If, on the other hand, you would like to try your hand yourself, darts is widely played in bars and cafés around the city.

Football

Ajax
Amsterdam ArenA, Bijlmermeer; tel: 020 311 1444; www.ajax.nl/ travel; Metro: Strandvliet
Amsterdam's Ajax is one of the top European clubs. Home matches are played at the ArenA, in the southeastern part of the city. Tickets can be bought at the gate or booked

Left: the most Amsterdamisch activity – and means of tranport.

In addition, if it's cold enough, you can skate on the canals or at the seasonal skating rink in the Museumplein. SEE ALSO FESTIVALS AND EVENTS, P.51

Swimming

Het Marnix
Marnixplein 1; tel: 020 5246 000; www.hetmarnix.nl; Mon–Thur 7am–10pm, Fri 7am–6pm, Sat–Sun 7am–8pm; Tram: 3; map p.130 A3

Health centre with two pools, plus Jacuzzis and saunas. Naturist evening on Tuesdays.

De Mirandabad
De Mirandalaan 9; tel: 020 546 4444; www.mirandabad.nl; Mon–Fri 7am–10pm, Sat–Sun 10am–5pm; Tram: 25; Bus: 15, 169

Pool complex featuring a stone beach, wave machine, waterslide, whirlpool and outdoor pool (May–Aug). Also has squash courts, a fitness centre and restaurant.

Sloterparkbad
President Allendelaan 3; tel: 020 506 3506; www.sloterpark bad.nl; Mon–Fri 7am–10pm, Sat–Sun 9am–4pm; Tram: 14

Amsterdam's largest swimming pool complex, centred around a 50m (164ft) indoor pool. Outside, there is a water park and another pool.

Tennis

Amstelpark
Koenenkade 8, Amsterdamse Bos; tel: 020 301 0700; www.amstelpark.nl; Apr–Sept: Mon–Fri 8am–11pm, Sat–Sun 8am–9pm, Oct–Mar: Mon–Fri 8am–midnight, Sat–Sun 8am–11pm; Tram: 5; Bus: 142, 166, 170, 172

Sixteen indoor and 26 outdoor tennis courts (racket hire available). Also has a swimming pool and sauna.

in advance from the VVV or by writing to: Ajax Travel, p/a Packages, PO Box 12522, 1100 AM Amsterdam (fax: 311 1945; email: tickets@ ajax.nl). Groups of 10 or more can take a two-hour tour of the ArenA (tel: 311 1336 for reservations). The **Ajax Museum** (tel: 311 1444) is also worth visiting.

Hockey

The Dutch excel at hockey – the women's national team, in particular, is one of the best in the world, having won the World Cup six times. If you are visiting during the season (Sept–May) and would like to see a game, visit the **Wagener Stadium** in the **Amsterdamse Bos** (tel: 020 545 6107). If, on the other hand, it's ice hockey you are interested in, consult the NIJB website (www.nijb.nl) for fixtures during the season (Oct–Feb). The Amstel Tijgers (www.amsteltijgerspro.nl) are the main local team and play at the Jaap Edenhal (the indoor rink at the **Jaap Edenbaan Rink** – *see Ice-Skating, right*).

SEE ALSO PARKS AND GARDENS, P.102

Ice-Skating

Jaap Edenbaan Rink
64 Radioweg; tel: 020 694 9652; www.jaapeden.nl; Mon–Fri 1–3.45pm, Sat–Sun noon–4pm; Tram: 9

There is skating all year round on the indoor rink. On Saturday nights (8.40am–11.30pm) this is a disco on ice. In winter (Oct–Mar), you can also use the 400m (1,312ft) ice track outside (Mon, Thur–Fri 8am–4pm, 9–11pm, Tue 9.20am–4pm, 9–11pm, Wed 8am–4pm, Sat noon–4.30pm, 8.40–11.30pm, Sun 10.30am–5.30pm).

Below: replica Ajax gear for sale in a market.

Theatre and Dance

Classical theatre, mime, comedy, marionettes, improv, musicals, ballet, open-podium theatre and contemporary dance; Amsterdam offers just about every conceivable style of performance. There's variety, too, in the venues utilised, from venerable 18th-century theatres to post-industrial conversions and minimalist dance studios. To find out what's on, consult the papers and websites listed in *Essentials, p.48*. Seats can be booked through the AUB (26 Leidseplein; tel: 0900 0191; www.uitlijn.nl; daily 10am–6pm) or the VVV.

Theatre

Perhaps the best time of year to engage with Amsterdam's rich theatre scene is the summer. As well as offering the possibility of outdoor productions in the city's parks, there are also several important festivals. In early June there is the **Holland Festival**. Then, later in the month, is the **International Theatre School Festival** (www.its festival.nl). And finally, in July, there is the **Over Het Ij Festival** (www.overhetij.nl) of fringe theatre at various venues in Amsterdam Noord.

SEE ALSO FESTIVALS AND EVENTS, P.51

COMPANIES AND VENUES

Amsterdam Marionetten Theater
Nieuwe Jonkerstraat 8; tel: 020 620 8027; www.marionetten theater.nl; Tram: 4, 9; Metro: Nieuwmarkt; map p.137 C1
Mozart and Offenbach operas performed by puppets.

Amsterdam RAI Theater
Europaplein 8–22; tel: 020 549 1212; www.raitheater.nl; NS Amsterdam RAI
Large venue hosting opera, ballet, theatre and musical spectaculars.

Het Compagnietheater
Kloveniersburgwal 50; tel: 020 520 5320; www.theater compagnie.nl; Tram: 4, 9, 14, 16, 24, 25; map p.136 C3
This is a major company for serious theatre productions.

De Engelenbak
Nes 17; tel: 020 626 68 66; www.engelenbak.nl; Tram: 4, 9, 14, 16, 24, 25; map p.136 B2
Theatre devoted to am-dram. Features the long-running *Open Bak* (Tue 8.30pm), where anyone can get up and strut their stuff.

Frascati
Nes 63; tel: 020 751 6400; www.indenes.nl; Tram: 4, 9, 16, 24, 25; map p.136 B3

Although most theatre performances are in Dutch, Amsterdam is putting on more English-speaking events year-round. The VVV publishes brochures promoting these Amsterdam Arts Adventures in summer and winter. In addition, during the Holland Festival in June each year, numerous foreign companies perform in different languages.

Progressive theatre by up-and-coming actors and directors. The former Gasthuis Theater merged with Frascati in 2008. Many performances in English or without words.

De Kleine Komedie
Amstel 56–58; tel: 020 624 0534; www.dekleinekomedie.nl; Tram: 4, 9, 14, 16, 25; map p.136 B4
Grand old theatre built in 1786 presents comedy, cabaret and musical shows.

Koninklijk Theater Carré
Amstel 115–125; tel: 0900 252 5255; www.theatercarre.nl; Tram: 4, 6, 7, 10; map p.134 B3
Nineteenth-century theatre hosts touring productions of musicals and comedy.

Melkweg
Lijnbaansgracht 234a; tel: 020 531 8181; www.melkweg.nl; Tram: 1, 2, 5, 10; map p.133 D2
Arts centre accommodating theatre and dance productions as well as a cinema.
SEE ALSO MUSIC, P.92

Stadsschouwburg
Leidseplein 26; tel: 020 624 2311; www.ssba.nl; Tram: 1, 2, 5, 6, 7, 10; map p.133 D2

Right: puppets in action at the Marionetten Theater.

Left: *Spiegel* in performance at the Stadsschouwburg.

Hetveem Theater
Van Diemenstraat 410; tel: 020 626 9291; www.hetveem theater.nl; Tram: 3; Bus: 18, 21, 22, 49; map p.130 B1
Former warehouse hosts mime and dance productions.

International Danstheater
Kloveniersburgwal 87; tel: 020 623 9112; www.intdans theater.nl; Tram: 4, 9, 16, 24, 25; map p.136 B3
Presents shows by major choreographers incorporating dance from around the world.

KIT Tropentheater
Kleine Zaal Linnaeusstraat 2; Grote Zaal Mauritskade 63; tel: 020 568 8500; www.tropen theater.nl; Tram: 3, 7, 9, 10, 14; Bus: 22; map p.135 D3
Next door to the **Tropen-museum** *(see Museums and Galleries, p.88)*, this theatre presents concerts and dance from India, Africa, the Far East and South America.

Muiderpoorttheater
Tweede van Swindenstraat 26; tel: 020 668 1313; www. muiderpoorttheater.nl; Tram: 3, 7, 9, 10, 14; map p.135 D3
Presents productions by international touring artists.

Muziektheater
Amstel 3; tel: 020 625 5455; www.muziektheater.nl; box office: Mon–Sat 10am–6pm, Sun 11.30am–2.30pm (on concert days box office stays open until the curtain goes up); Tram: 9, 14; map p.137 C4
The sumptuous 1,600-seat Muziektheater, opened in 1986, is home to the National Ballet and Netherlands Opera. There are usually free half-hour performances on Tuesday afternoons. The ballet, under the direction of Wayne Eagling, offers a repertoire of classics as well as recent work by top choreographers.

For two weeks each July, the **Julidans Festival** (www. julidans.nl) welcomes some of the world's biggest names in contemporary dance at various venues across the city.

Shows everything from classical theatre to ballet to contemporary comedy.

Theater het Amsterdamse Bos
Amsterdamse Bos; tel: 020 643 3286; www.bostheater.nl; Bus: 66, 170, 172, 199; map p.133 D4
Classic theatre in the park on summer evenings.
SEE ALSO PARKS AND GARDENS, P.102

Theater Fabriek Amsterdam
Czaar Peterstraat 213; tel: 522 5260; www.theaterfabriek amsterdam.nl; Tram: 10, 26;

Bus: 42, 43
Post-industrial building converted into a theatre for musical extravaganzas.

Dance

Holland's foremost dance companies are the **Dutch National Ballet**, based at the Muziektheater in Amsterdam, and the **Netherlands Dance Theater**, based in The Hague. In addition, famous names to look out for include the choreographers Anouk van Dijk, Hans Hof, Ohad Naharin and Pieter de Tuiter.

COMPANIES AND VENUES
DWA-Studio Theatre
Arie Biemondstraat 107b; tel: 020 689 1789; www.danswerkplaats. nl; Tram: 1, 17; map p.132 C3
Young talent brings fresh life to modern dance.

Transport

Thanks to its compact, easy-to-navigate City Centre, Amsterdam is easily explored by foot or on two wheels – cycling being a great way to get an authentic local vantage point. Those who do utilise the public transport system will find that nowhere in the city is ever far away, thanks to the extensive, integrated tram, bus and metro network that operates daily from 6am to 12.30am, before night buses take over. However, perhaps the most evocative means of getting around is by water, with boat tours, ferries, rented pedalos and electric motorboats allowing visitors to soak up the atmosphere and sights from the city's famous canals.

Getting There

BY RAIL

There are good rail connections to Amsterdam from Brussels, Paris, Antwerp, Cologne, Berlin and the North Sea ports. The **Eurostar** Channel Tunnel train travels from London St Pancras to Brussels, from where trains run to Amsterdam. It takes about six hours from London. The Thalys high-speed train (reservation required) connects the city with Brussels, Paris and Cologne.
Eurostar: tel: 08705 186 186 (in UK); www.eurostar.com
Rail Europe: tel: 08448 484 064 (in UK); www.raileurope.co.uk
Thalys: tel: 0900 9296 (in the Netherlands); www.thalys.com

BY AIR

Schiphol Airport lies 15 km (9 miles) southwest of Amsterdam. There are almost hourly services during the day between Amsterdam and the UK. Direct daily flights exist between Schiphol and US and Canadian destinations; daily flights also operate from Australia and New Zealand. There are regular links with all major European airports.

The 24-hour rail service from Schiphol to Amsterdam Centraal Station, with up to five trains an hour at peak times, takes about 20 minutes.

The Connexxion hotel shuttle bus from Schiphol runs every 20–30 minutes, serving over 100 city hotels from 6am–9pm, although it is twice as expensive as the train. Taxis to the City Centre leave from in front of Schiphol Plaza and cost around €45.

BY SEA

From the UK, **Stena Line** operates two ferries a day (for passengers with vehicles) from Harwich to Hoek van Holland: crossing time is 7½ hours. **P&O Ferries** sail daily from Hull to Rotterdam, taking 12 hours.
Stena Line: tel: 0870 570 7070 (UK); www.stenaline.com
P&O Ferries: tel: 0871 664 5645 (UK); www.poferries.com

BY COACH

Generally the cheapest way of reaching the Netherlands, **Eurolines/National Express** (tel: 08717 818 181; www.eurolines.com) operate frequent coach services to Amsterdam from the UK.

BY CAR

From the UK, the Channel Tunnel provides a 35-minute drive-on service from Folkestone to Calais, where there is a motorway connection to Amsterdam through Belgium. Journey time from Calais is about four hours.

From Hoek van Holland to Amsterdam, driving time is roughly 2½ hours. To drive in the Netherlands, you must carry a current EU or national driving licence, vehicle registration document, valid MOT and insurance.

Getting Around

BY BUS, METRO AND TRAM

Strip tickets *(Strippenkarten)*

Canal Buses pick up passengers at 14 stops along three different routes, taking you to museums and tourist attractions. A one-day hop-on-hop-off bus pass is €18 (tel: 623 9886; www.canal.nl).

Left: a tram makes its way from the City Centre.

electric-powered motorboat yourself. Rent these from:
Canal Motorboats:
Zandhoek 10a; tel: 422 7007
Sesa Rent a Boat:
2 Stuurmankade, Borneo-Eiland; tel: +31 06 4855 6819

BY BICYCLE

Amsterdam has numerous bike lanes; to experience the city like the locals, get around by bike. Watch out for tram tracks: they should only be crossed at right angles!
Damstraat Rent-a-bike
20–22 Damstraat; tel: 625 5029
MacBike
2 Mr Visserplein; tel: 620 0985
Hire bikes from these two companies.
SEE ALSO ENVIRONMENT, P.45
Yellow Bike
29 Nieuwezijds Kolk; tel: 620 6940
Offers group tours of the city.
Mike's Bike Tours
134 Kerkstraat; tel: 622 7970
These extend outside the city.

BY TAXI

Cabs can be found at key locations (in front of Centraal Station, at Leidseplein, the Dam and Waterlooplein), or by calling 0900 677 7777. Meters are used and the cost depends on the zone and the time of day. You can also use the **Water Taxi** in front of Centraal Station (tel: 535 6363).

BY CAR

Parking on the streets within Amsterdam's ring road A10 requires you to buy tickets at street vending machines, marked with a 'P'. However, it is notoriously difficult to find a parking space, and the city is known for high fines and parking clamps. Park-and-ride schemes are located on the city's outskirts.

are stamped every time you use the bus, tram or metro, are cheaper than single tickets and can be bought in lots of 15 or 45. The city is divided into zones, and you cancel one strip more than the number of zones you travel within – for example, two strips for one zone, three strips for two zones. Buy tickets from the **GVB Tickets & Info** office on the Stationsplein opposite Centraal Station, metro stations and tourist offices.

The **Stop/Go** minibus service runs between Waterlooplein, Centraal Station and Oosterdork daily every 12 minutes from 9am–5.30pm. With no fixed stops on the route, hold out your hand to indicate you want to board. Strip and GVB 1-, 2- and 3-day tickets are valid, otherwise tickets can be bought from the driver.

On the metro you must stamp your ticket in the machines provided.

The tram is the best means of getting around the City Centre. Tickets must be

Right: one of the best ways to see the city is from the water.

stamped by the conductor at, or towards, the rear, or in the machines next to the doors. If you have no ticket, enter through the front door and buy a ticket from the driver.

BY BOAT

Maps and routes for canal pedalos (or waterbikes) are provided by the hire companies, located opposite Centraal Station, the Anne Frank Huis and opposite the Rijksmuseum. For information: tel: 020 623 9886; www.canal.nl/en.

It is also possible to navigate the canals in a traditional *rondvaart*, on a canal boat tour, or by hiring a small,

Walks, Bike Rides and Canal Tours

A msterdam is a city that it is easy to walk around, with most of the major attractions packed into the small City Centre. It can be confusing, but provided you have a good map and a reasonable sense of direction you shouldn't go far wrong. However, it is a city that's famous for its canals and its bicycles, so taking a canal tour or a bicycle tour, or simply hiring a bike of your own, are other ideal ways of seeing the city. Meanwhile, joining an organised tour is a way of discovering lesser-known parts of this fascinating place.

By Bike

Follow the Yellow Bike Road
Nieuwezijds Kolk 29; tel: 020 620 6940; www.yellowbike.nl; Tram: 4, 9, 16; map p.136 B1
As well as renting bikes to the braver souls, Yellow Bike also runs guided bike tours both in Amsterdam and out to the surrounding countryside. It can be a great and easy way to get out of the city, without having to do all the organising yourself, and takes you to the Waterland district north of Amsterdam. The city tour takes in all the major sights, and they last for a good three hours, though there is time for a rest as you visit places ranging from Rembrandt's House to the inevitable Red Light District. There are usually two tours a day, every day, and they must be booked in advance.

On Foot

In the Red Light District
Prostitutes Information Centre; Enge Kerksteeg 3; tel: 020 420 7328; www.pic-amsterdam.com; Tram: 4, 9, 16; map p.136 C1

Above: queuing to board a canal boat.

If you're nervous about visiting the Red Light District, or are curious to know what really goes on behind the curtains, these tours led by a former prostitute really do give a genuine insight into Amsterdam's sex industry. It's a highly regulated business, and while these tours are not for the shy they are genuinely fascinating about this aspect of Amsterdam life. Tours are every Saturday evening and must be booked ahead. Another option is to arrange to have dinner at one of the city's notorious sex clubs, with a

chance to also meet the performers afterwards. See the website or phone for up-to-date details.

Mee in Mokum
Keizersgracht 346; tel: 020 625 1390; Tram: 13, 14, 17; map p.133 D1
You need to telephone to book a tour through this long-established organisation, which runs walking tours that are led by local residents. Obviously most walking tours are led by local people, but these are long-time inhabitants of the city, who give more informal touts of the Amster-

Left: enjoy some of the best city views from two wheels.

hard to beat and the standard is first-class.

Free Canal Trips

Leidseplein 12; www.amsterdam boatclub.com; Tram: 1, 2, 5; map p.133 D2

The members of the St Nicolaas Boat Club started giving their free canal rides in 1997. They do accept donations, and they empha-sise their trips are about enjoying the canals and relaxing, so you're advised to bring food and drink along with you. They're very informal and numbers are kept quite small, so as it's a first-come first-served basis, you need to go along to their office inside the Boom Chicago comedy venue on Leidseplein and sign up. Boats leave from nearby, and there are usually 1–2 a day in winter and 3–4 a day in summer, in the afternoons and evenings. These aren't glitzy glass-topped tourist cruises, but are in open *tuindersvletten*, or 'garden flats', the traditional boats for carrying vegetables and animals around the canals.

dam they know, principally in the Jordaan and Old Centre districts.

Rembrandt Mystery Tours

www.letsgo-amsterdam.com; Metro: Centraal Station; map p.131 C3

These tours are really differ-ent, revealing some of the lesser-known aspects of Rembrandt's fascinating life, as well as the city locations with Rembrandt links. They range from graveyards to the Red Light District, and run daily from September to June. The same company, Let's Go, also runs more wide-ranging Mystery Tours of Amsterdam, showing the city's more macabre side, as well as decidedly non-macabre bicycle tours of the nearby Dutch country-side of windmills, tulips and Edam cheese.

On the Water

Dinner Boat Cruises

Prinsengracht 391; tel: 020 330 1910; www.classicboat dinners.nl; Tram: 13, 14, 17;

map p.133 D1

They're kitsch, they're corny and they seem like a tourist cliché, but a romantic dinner cruise around Amsterdam's canals is still a fabulous experience. These particular cruises take place on a lux-urious restored 1905 boat, the *Kleijn Amsterdam*, and with a six-course gourmet dinner and wines, they are not cheap. But if you want to do something special, with someone special, they're

Right: looking down from the Westerkerk tower.

Some of the best views of Amsterdam are easily reached as they're in some of the city's major attractions. Climb to the top of the tower of the Westerkerk *(see Churches and Synagogues, p.39)*, which is the tallest church tower in the city, for probably the finest view. Not far behind is the tower of the Zuiderkerk, also with impres-sive views. Go up to the roof of the NEMO Museum too *(see Museums and Galleries, p.89)*, for a good look over Amsterdam's waterfront and skyline.

Atlas

The following streetplan of Amsterdam makes it easy to find the attractions listed in the A–Z section. A selective index to streets and sights will help you find other locations throughout the city.

Map Legend

Motorway	Railway
Dual carriageway	Metro
Main road	Bus station
Minor road	Car ferry
Footpath	Airport
Pedestrian area	Tourist information
Notable building	Sight of interest
Transport hub	Cathedral / church
Park	Temple
Hotel	Synagogue
Urban area	Statue / monument
Non urban area	Windmill

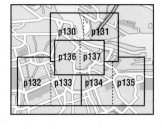

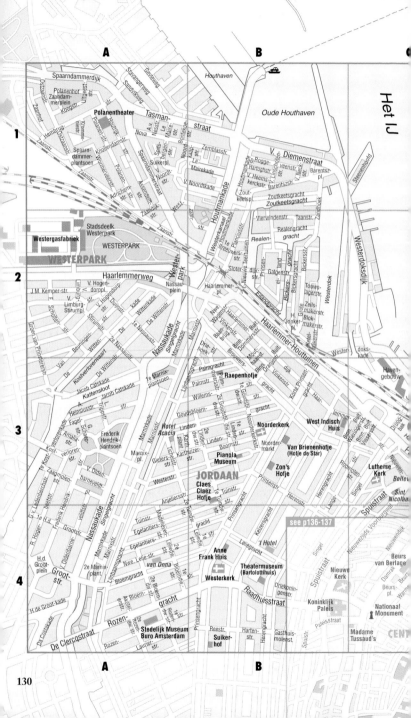

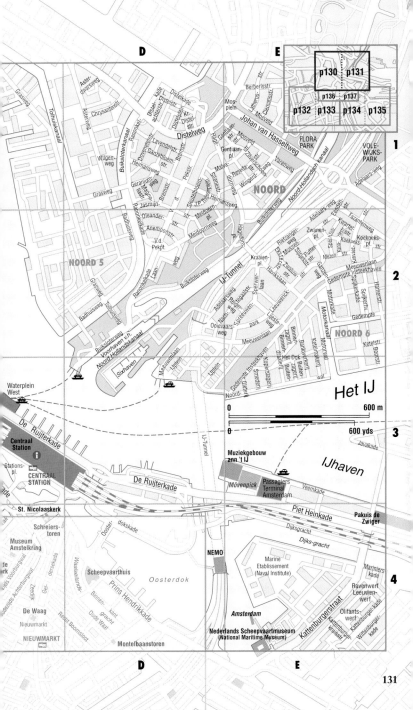

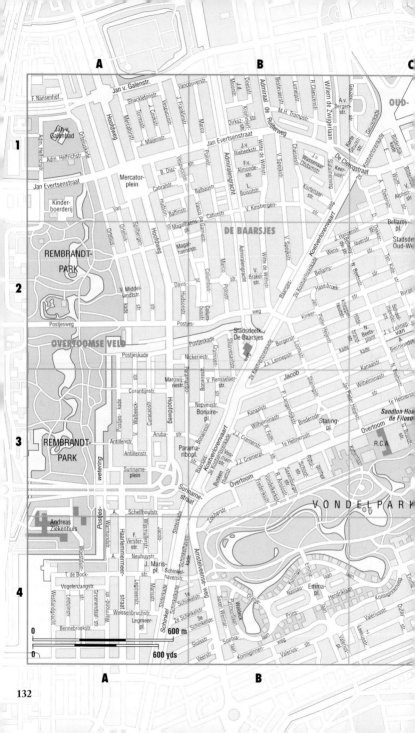

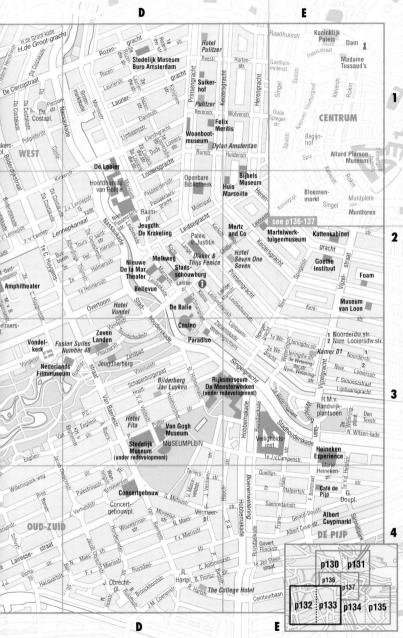

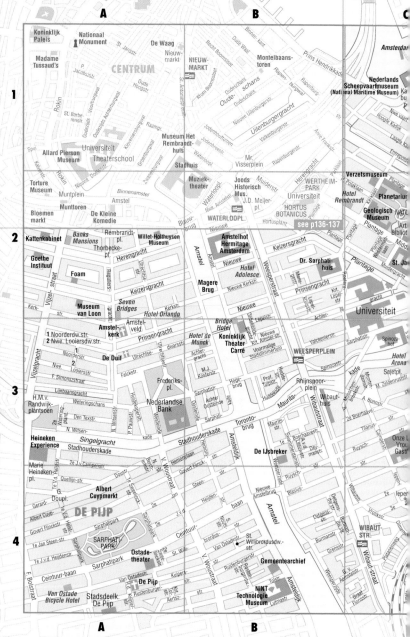

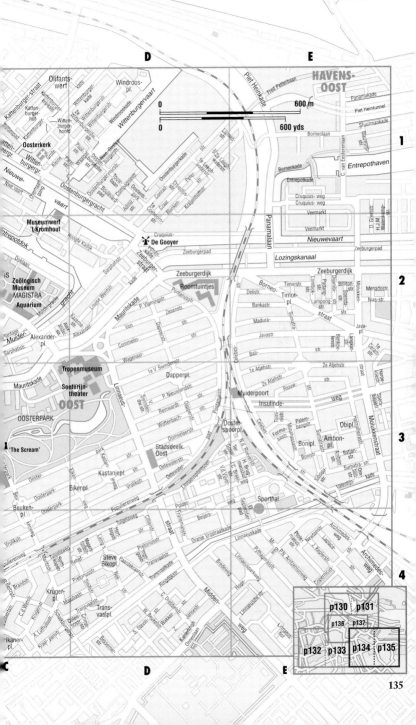

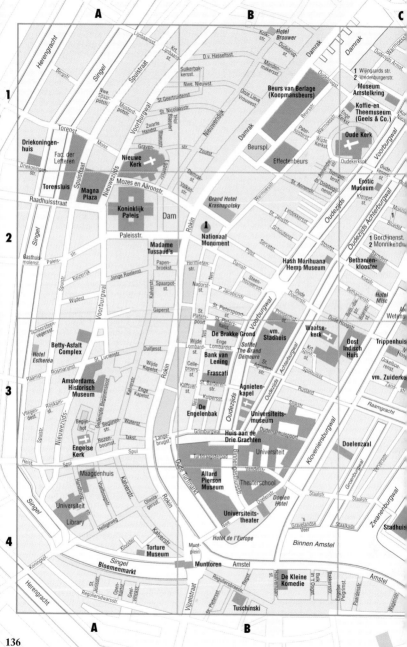

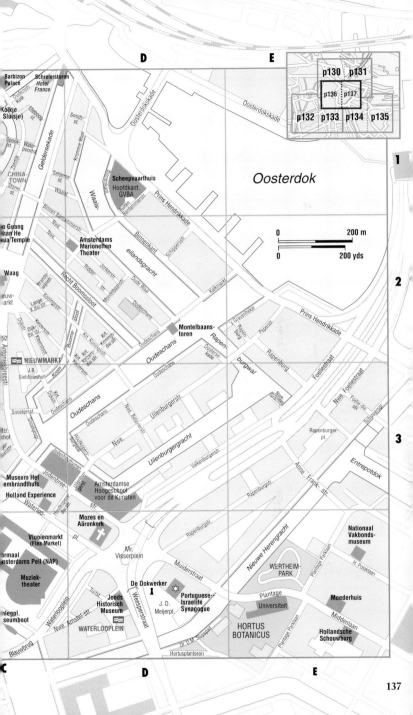

Street Atlas Index

Index

Insight Smart Guide: Amsterdam
Compiled by: Mike Gerrard, Michael Macaroon, Austin Clark, Lara Dunston and Terry Carter
Edited by: Sarah Sweeney
Proofread and indexed by: Neil Titman
All photography by: Greg Gladman/APA except: Banks Mansion 67; Allard Bovenberg 80C; Maarten Brinkgreve 82/83B; eatdrinksleep.com 64C; Anne Frank House 80B; Fusion Suites 68/69T; Fu Works/The Kobal Collection/ Vrenegoor, Jaap 53B; Gunter Glaner/Seven Bridges Hotel 69BL&BR; Vincent van Gogh Foundation 5CL, 78/79T, 86; Hans van Heeswijk 87T; Dirk Hol 63BR; Holland.com 5C, 50/51(all), 85; Kamer01 64/65T; Liselore Kamping 87C&B; leonardo.com 65B, 66T&C, 71C&B; Jo Misdom 123B; Movenpick Hotels & Resorts 70T&C; Museum Tramlijn 84B; Museum Van Loon 82T; Science Center

NEMO 89; Jean-Pierre Stoop 122/123T; Sarah Sweeney 84T; Verzetsmuseum Amsterdam 88B; Woonbootmuseum 81
Picture Manager: Steven Lawrence
Maps: Mapping Ideas Ltd
Series Editor: Jason Mitchell

First Edition 2009
© 2009 Apa Publications GmbH & Co. Verlag KG Singapore Branch, Singapore.
Printed in Singapore by Insight Print Services (Pte) Ltd
Worldwide distribution enquiries:
Apa Publications GmbH & Co. Verlag KG (Singapore Branch) 38 Joo Koon Road, Singapore 628990; tel: (65) 6865 1600; fax: (65) 6861 6438
Distributed in the UK and Ireland by:
GeoCenter International Ltd
Meridian House, Churchill Way West, Basingstoke, Hampshire RG21 6YR; tel: (44 1256) 817 987; fax: (44 1256) 817 988

Distributed in the United States by:
Langenscheidt Publishers, Inc.
36–36 33rd Street 4th Floor, Long Island City, New York 11106; tel: (1 718) 784 0055; fax: (1 718) 784 0640I
Contacting the Editors
We would appreciate it if readers would alert us to errors or outdated information by writing to: Apa Publications, PO Box 7910, London SE1 1WE, UK; fax: (44 20) 7403 0290; e-mail: insight@apaguide.co.uk
No part of this book may be reproduced, stored in a retrieval system or transmitted in any form or by any means (electronic, mechanical, photocopying, recording or otherwise), without prior written permission of Apa Publications. Brief text quotations with use of photographs are exempted for book review purposes only. Information has been obtained from sources believed to be reliable, but its accuracy and completeness, and the opinions based thereon, are not guaranteed.

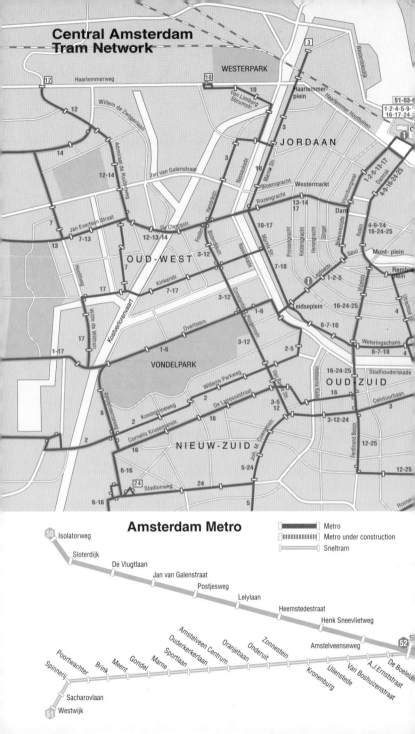